THE TEN COMMANDMENTS
AND THE DECLINE OF THE WEST

The Ten Commandments and the Decline of the West

ROB WARNER

KINGSWAY PUBLICATIONS
EASTBOURNE

Biblical quotations are taken from the
New International Version © 1973, 1978, 1984 by the
International Bible Society.

ISBN 0 85476 677 4

Co-published in South Africa with
SCB Publishers
Cornelis Struik House, 80 McKenzie Street
Cape Town 8001, South Africa.
Reg no 04/02203/06

Designed and produced by Bookprint Creative Services
P.O. Box 827, BN21 3YJ, England for
KINGSWAY PUBLICATIONS LTD
Lottbridge Drove, Eastbourne, East Sussex BN23 6NT.
Printed in Great Britain.

This book is dedicated to Clive Calver,
eloquent and tireless defender of the faith
and ardent exponent of biblical morality.
The entire evangelical movement in the UK
is greatly in his debt.

Contents

Acknowledgements

My special thanks go to my wife, Claire, who somehow manages to combine working as a deputy head, being a mum to our two sons and keeping me going, in preaching, travelling and writing. I am grateful for all the support, friendship, prayer and encouragement we consistently receive at Queen's Road Church, Wimbledon. I am grateful to the think-tank team at our church, who brainstormed their way through the Commandments with me, providing me with many fresh and stimulating perspectives on the foundational wisdom of these ancient ethical precepts for the well-being not only of individuals but of an entire society. I am especially grateful to Debbie Haine, whose organisational, research and analytical skills and determined efforts to keep other demands on my time at bay when I am writing to a deadline, have helped keep me sane. Special thanks must also go to Premier Radio, who provided me with a complete set of daily newspapers for several months, while I broadcast their daily news review. I am also indebted to the statistical data compiled by the Maranatha Community, the Movement for Christian Democracy, Christian Aid and TEAR Fund. Thanks finally go to Alan Johnson, who was able to provide me with some useful background research commissioned by Spring Harvest.

The horror! The horror! . . .
It would have been too dark – too dark altogether . . .

J. Conrad, *The Heart of Darkness*, 1902

Things fall apart; the centre cannot hold;
Mere anarchy is loosed upon the world,
The blood-dimmed tide is loosed, and everywhere
The ceremony of innocence is drowned;
The best lack all conviction, while the worst
Are full of passionate intensity.

W.B. Yeates, *The Second Coming*, 1921

Introduction

In an era of surging social upheaval, escalating crime rates and fears that society itself may be coming apart at the seams, there is a pressing need to re-evaluate the moral basis of Western society. Edmund Burke once observed, 'Men are qualified for civil liberty in exact proportion to their disposition to put moral chains upon their own appetites' (A letter to a member of the National Assembly, 1791). How very far removed from this perspective is the decadent self-indulgence of the late twentieth century, when the general consensus has been for some years that to 'do what comes naturally' is the true path to freedom and fulfilment.

While Alvin Toffler wrote persuasively about 'future shock', that is, cultural bewilderment and dislocation faced with the continually accelerating rate of change in modern society, another future prospect is now becoming predominant in our culture: future angst or future dread. Turn on any TV or radio station, open any newspaper and a mood of growing pessimism is not hard to find. On Friday 26 September, to cite a typical day, the morning debate on one TV station was child prostitution and the fact that a growing number of young girls, some as young as eleven, are working the streets in Britain and in great demand with the punters. Meanwhile on Radio 4 that same morning, concern was being expressed about the rapid increase in the number of children carrying knives or other dangerous weapons, one of the most fashionable in certain districts being a snooker ball wrapped in a strong sock. Searching and anxious questions are being voiced, both among friends and family and in the media: What kind of society are we becoming? What kind of world will our children's children inherit?

The Daily Telegraph summed up the results of a Gallup poll in June 1996 with the observation that British people 'are filled with unprecedented gloom about virtually every aspect of life' (*The Daily Telegraph*, Monday 3 June 1996). About half of those surveyed thought that standards are deteriorating in health (51%), education (47%) and happiness (53%). Three-quarters thought that standards of honesty are worsening (74%) and almost everyone considered standards of behaviour to be in decline (92%). Only 3% think we are getting more honest, and just 1% think our standards of behaviour are improving. Over all, just 3% say that peace of mind is better than in the past, while 76% say that they now have less peace of mind. This was one of the most bleak and pessimistic sets of results that Gallup had ever polled, and made John Major's quest for the 'feel good factor' look even more unlikely to succeed.

The next month, Gallup produced what the *Telegraph* called a morality poll (*The Daily Telegraph*, Friday 5 July 1996), in which 72% of adults said that it is now left too much up to individuals to devise their own moral code. Some 83% said their moral code came mainly from their parents, and 49% said that the church had failed to provide adequate moral guidance to the nation. The overwhelming majority thought that schools should be teaching tolerance of others (95%) and respect for people in authority (93%). They also wanted schools to emphasise that it is wrong to drink and drive (95%) and also to tell lies (88%). As many as

71% still wanted schools to teach Christian values, although only 46% also wanted schools to teach Christian doctrine.

The most striking results concerned adultery and the general sense of the nation's moral health. When it comes to adultery, the old cultural consensus has clearly broken down: 47% thought adultery wrong in all circumstances, 44% thought it could be justified occasionally and 5% thought it could be justified frequently. Only 42% thought schools should teach the moral value of chastity before marriage, while 47% did not want the value of chastity to be upheld any longer. As to the moral state of the nation, 75% think that Britain is less moral today than it was fifty years ago. The recognition of moral decay is now extensive and acute. Taking these polls together, we are faced with a nation of rapidly declining moral standards, more dishonesty and poorer standards of behaviour. Acceptance of adultery as a fact of life is at an all-time high, but happiness and peace of mind have never been so hard to find. Many have concluded that we are entering a period that will be marked by a great deal of soul-searching: what cultural or moral choices have brought us to such a condition?

T.S. Eliot observed that ours has become the first society to attempt to live without reference to God. The result has been an experiment not only in religion but also in morality, because the abandonment of an absolute deity leads in time to the abandonment of moral absolutes and the gradual decay of a moral consensus in society. There can be no final sense of right and wrong, good and evil, without an absolute reference point from which this moral framework is derived. As a result we have inevitably embraced a pattern of moral relativism, in which everyone does what is right in their own eyes . . . so long as it causes no offence or harm to the powerful.

At the end of the twentieth century we can begin to assess the consequences of this experiment in ethics, and the evidence is hardly encouraging. While Nietzsche confidently argued that men and women would truly be free when the constraints of Christian morality were overthrown, the truth is that never have Western people looked so enchained. Selfish actions have multiple consequences, most of them negative. Many are experiencing a steadily increasing fear that Western society is in the process of becoming a seething mass of unpredictable consequences in a generation beset with selfish living.

The Great War of 1914–1918 shattered the optimistic hope of late-nineteenth-century evolutionism (a view of human society only tangentially related to the Darwinian theory of evolution) that the advance of the species and of Western capitalism would make unhindered progress. When the alternative, idealistic aspirations of Marxism collapsed into the totalitarianism of the so-called dictatorship of the proletariat, the political history of the early twentieth century provoked a number of novelists to create dystopian visions of the future, notably George Orwell's *Nineteen Eighty-Four*, Aldous Huxley's *Brave New World* and Yevgeny Zamyatin's *We*. As we draw near to the new millennium, we can expect an increasing number of artists to create apocalyptic visions of the death and collapse of Western culture and society. TV screens are likely to feature with increasing regularity soul-searching studies of the twentieth century. Where did we go so very wrong, losing the kind of coherent and agreed moral framework that any civilisation needs if it is to survive and prosper?

This debate about the nation's morality was given new prominence in January 1996, when Nicholas Tate, the director of the School Curriculum and Assessment Authority, expressed the intention to consult widely concerning the shared values that schools should be expected to transmit to children. Tate appeared to be suggesting that moral and spiritual values are an intrinsic part of our culture and therefore need to be integrated into the National Curriculum rather than be given minimal attention at the margins of our education system, left to wither through neglect. This represents a monumental shift of emphasis. For many years the dominant trend among intellectuals and educators has been to seek to eliminate talk of morality and spirituality from public discourse. They have been relegated to the minor status of private matters that would constitute an irrelevant and inappropriate intrusion into those forums that have received their agenda from post-Enlightenment scientific materialism, namely education, politics and current affairs.

George Carey, the Archbishop of Canterbury, took up the baton of this moral debate in a landmark speech in the House of Lords in July 1996. He spoke of the rich moral legacy of the Judaeo-Christian tradition and the danger that we might be in the process of squandering this inheritance. His detractors were immediate and many. One peer denounced any such talk as a 'self-indulgent farce', asserting that morality is a private matter and should be left to the conscience of individuals. *The Times* regretted that when the Archbishop warned of a business culture moving from 'trust, integrity and responsibility' to a new world of 'chaotic gangsterism' his language had been too colourful and tabloid. Others mocked his mild-mannered protestations, and in particular his refusal to comment upon the public confessions of adultery by both Prince Charles and Princess Diana. This exposed him to accusations, as John Casey expressed it in *The Times*, of being 'mealy-mouthed and insincere'.

Jonathan Sacks, the Chief Rabbi, was more supportive, noting that many social commentators have in recent years begun to emphasise that a moral framework is a necessary foundation for the future well-being of our society. (He cited American academics, Michael Sandel's *Democracy's Discontent*, James Q. Wilson's *The Moral Sense* and Alasdair MacIntyre's *Beyond Virtue*, and also British political analysts as diverse as John Gray, Melanie Phillips and Roger Scruton.) According to Sacks, the great and decisive contribution of the Judaeo-Christian tradition to the current debate is that it emphatically defends the place of a moral framework that goes beyond private, personal morality: 'It talks unashamedly of good and evil, duty and fidelity, love and obedience. It suggests that not all choices are equal: some lead on to blessing, others to lives of quiet despair' (*The Times*, Friday 5 July 1996).

In September 1996, Baroness Thatcher added her voice to the debate with a lecture at the Institute of United States Studies in London. She denounced the declining moral standards of Britain and in particular the massed ranks of muggers, petty burglars and terrorists that had made everyone feel 'less secure than we of a right should be'. Almost daily, she warned, we are faced with people for whom the words 'justice' and 'right' have no meaning. 'We have witnessed a coarsening of everything from art to music to literature to film. But for some people there seems to be nothing beyond the pale – for them freedom has no limits. The younger generation is being reared in a morally corrosive atmosphere where they are taught that in the name of liberty anything goes.' Inevitably for a politician of such resolute conservatism, Lady Thatcher could not resist also denouncing socialism and the European Union in the same lecture. None the less she struck a chord with many, and not merely among her own unwavering devotees, when she thundered against a debased culture that clamours for ever more licentiousness.

Mary Robinson, President of Eire and widely tipped as a future Secretary-General of the United Nations, has roundly declared: 'We need a new global ethic' (*Independent*, 4 June 1996). Swiss theologian Hans Küng has also affirmed the need for governments and businesses to accept an international moral framework to shape their policies and actions. The InterAction Council, an international gathering of former presidents and prime ministers, has proposed that in 1998, on the anniversary of the Universal Declaration of Human Rights, the United Nations should consider the possibility of issuing a Declaration of Human Obligations.

In all this debate one note continues to be sounded, by believers and non-believers alike – the need for a definite and clear moral framework which ensures that neither we nor our children lose sight of the fundamental distinction between right and wrong. Maybe the real issue is not how to create a new ethical framework, but how to reactivate the one we already have. The Judaeo-Christian tradition has consistently spoken with a united voice. The Ten Commandments represent not merely a fascinating snapshot of ancient morality, or the definitive summation of a primitive ethicist's life work. In their acceptance is the hope of a civilisation reborn. In their abandonment lie the consequences found in the bleak headlines and opinion polls of newspapers at the end of the twentieth century. Sartre once declared that hell is other people (*L'enfer c'est les autres – Huis Clos*): the repudiation of the Ten Commandments has begun to lead us towards nothing less than hell on earth.

This book is written as an appeal to take the Ten Commandments seriously once again. It does not merely assert the authority of revelation, insisting on an acceptance of these commandments because Jews and Christians believe that God has declared them. I have sought to explore a reasoned apologetic for each commandment. Two fundamental questions are often in sight. What are the practical consequences for our society if we fail to apply these commandments? And is it really possible that we could begin to restore these values today? It is my solemn conviction that this ancient moral code represents the best hope for re-establishing a decent and civilised society in the new millennium.

1

I am the Lord your God,
who brought you out of Egypt,
out of the land of slavery.
You shall have no other gods before me.

Deuteronomy 5: 6-7

The First Commandment
No Other Gods

To the modern mind, the commandments seem to begin in the wrong place. While innumerable commentators have suggested that our society needs to return to the Ten Commandments, what they usually mean is that we need to recover general agreement that the last six commandments, or at least some of them, are a necessary foundation for a society that is orderly, civilised and safe. In a modern, sophisticated, pluralistic society, in which any necessary link between religion and morality is often strenuously denied, the first four commandments would appear to be superfluous – at best optional extras, at worst arrogant and divisive. Can there be any lasting value and relevance in commandments about the place of spirituality and faith?

When George Carey proposed in the House of Lords that our society urgently needs to return to a framework of moral absolutes, there was much public assent, but also an outcry in the media. The correspondence columns in national newspapers were inflamed with righteous – and yet irreligious – indignation. Surely, many critics protested, the Archbishop was not seriously suggesting that religious people were more moral than unbelievers? Many atheists uphold a moral code. Religion has often been a spur not to higher morality but to greater immorality, most notably in the case of the crusades and other religious wars. Any suggestion that all practising Christians are superior in their behaviour to all unbelievers entirely lacks credibility, for while some believers are shining examples of love and self-sacrifice, others demonstrate a sheen of hypocrisy, sectarianism and negativity.

The virtue of tolerance

Our culture has come to assume that in religious beliefs and practices there is only one acceptable absolute: tolerance above all else. There is great value in such an approach. In a pluralistic society, it is essential that different ethnic and religious groups learn to tolerate approaches to life that are quite different and distinct from one another. We have had to learn together how to develop a culture of diversity, which comes to celebrate and enjoy different approaches to life, rather than imposing a rigid conformity. This has not been an easy process, and there are still many who hanker for the old days: an England where white men play cricket in mid-summer while their wives make cucumber sandwiches, or the old cultural homogeneity of the WASP governing élite in the United States – white, Anglo-Saxon, Protestant – and, naturally, male.

The limits to this diversity and tolerance are uncomfortably indistinct. There has been much debate in recent years as to whether certain notorious Islamic extremists should be allowed to live in Britain as refugees and exercise freedom of speech in mass rallies that incite hatred within the Muslim community. These leaders' convictions are expressly anti-democratic and anti-Semitic and so, should they ever come to power in their own countries, they would be sure to prohibit the freedom of speech and right of public assembly that they presently enjoy and exploit in Britain. As to Christians, religious imperialism has at last been widely recognised as a reprehensible contradiction of the gospel of Christ. When South American Indians agreed to baptism under the threat of the conquistadors' swords, they were merely surrendering to the might of their Spanish conquerors, and their forced baptisms were no more than a meaningless outward conformity. Faith in Jesus Christ must be chosen personally, without duress, physical or emotional, or it cannot be living faith at all.

Tolerance is a healthy expression of respect for those with whom we disagree. Far better to be in dialogue with those who hold different convictions than to denounce or silence them. But honest and open dialogue need not require an abandonment of core convictions. For some church leaders, dialogue with other religions begins from the assumption that there are no non-negotiables. A new lowest common denominator religion is being concocted out of the blandest ingredients of the great world faiths. For others, dialogue not only improves mutual understanding, but is also a forum in which to present and explain a particular set of convictions with both graciousness and clarity.

To say that a national economy would greatly benefit from a continuing dialogue between politicians and leaders from business and the trade unions is to promote tolerance and co-operation. But it would be naïve in the extreme to suppose that such mutually tolerant dialogue could ever lead to the various interest groups abandoning their own convictions and agreeing entirely with one another. Between a *dialogue of the bland*, in which no one is prepared to hold definite convictions, and a *dialogue of the deaf*, in which no one is prepared to hear and tolerate contrary convictions, it is vital that we cultivate a *dialogue of respect*, in religion as well as in politics.

While tolerance can be the beneficial product of pluralism, the common underlying assumptions of our society go further. Tolerance has become the highest virtue because the very possibility of absolute truth has been widely abandoned. Any attempt to persuade someone else to share your beliefs or moral convictions is seen as an unjustifiable intrusion into personal and private matters. Religious and moral convictions have been individualised. If you happen to hold certain convictions, and they help you live happily, then so much the better. But never presume that these convictions are applicable to anyone else, for these are aspects of life best kept to oneself. In a world of absolute tolerance, all truth is relative and no one has the right to impose their truth claims concerning religion and morality on anyone else. Religion is tolerated as privately engaging for those who happen to be religious. But religion is excluded from the public domain as essentially irrelevant.

This strange ambiguity of private tolerance and public exclusion is seen very clearly in the media. In soaps, that compulsory daily bill of fare for great swathes of the population, positive, leading characters are never portrayed as Christian believers. Where there is a religious dimension to soaps – and often there is none at all – religion is usually at worst a con, at best boring and irrelevant. Religious characters habitually fit one of three categories: hypocrites, who impose on others a morality they disregard themselves; fanatics, who have lost all touch with rationality and reality – often the storyline is strengthened if the fanatics are also exposed as hypocrites; and thirdly, wimps – this type is usually played by a drip in a dog collar.

In documentaries and current affairs programmes, secular rationalism takes a different form. A distinctively Christian perspective on any issue of debate is habitually excluded. Where Christian spokespersons are involved, they run the risk of being patronised and marginalised, as if intelligent debate really has no place for a religious dimension or distinctively Christian insights. Other contributors may denigrate Christian values, but their prejudices and assertions often go unchallenged since they reinforce the prevailing cultural bias which assumes that Christianity is legitimately, even necessarily, excluded from serious, reasonable, contemporary debate about the future of the nation. The poor calibre and lack of media training of some church representatives certainly do not help, but the most significant factor in the marginalisation of Christian contributions to public debate is the cultural assumption that Christian faith and morality are intrinsically irrelevant to the development of Britain as a multi-cultural, pluralistic, post-modern society.

The fatal flaw

Relativism holds sway as the dominant cultural assumption in the West today, where the very notion of absolute truth and morality has been abandoned. However, the logic of relativism is fatally flawed. Relativism asserts that there is no such thing as absolute truth. But in making that statement, relativism promotes itself as the definitive, absolute truth that debars all other truth claims from being absolute. The implicit assertion of relativism is therefore that there is no such thing as absolute truth except for the proposition that there is no such thing as absolute truth. This is a statement guilty of self-contradiction. If the statement is true, it promptly destroys itself, by excluding the possibility of its being an absolute and definitive statement for all time!

The tyranny of dogmatic relativism must be exposed and repudiated. In past generations, many values and beliefs have been given an absolute status with a casual hastiness and an indifference to rigorous examination. With a similar casualness, our culture has sought to build upon the foundation of absolute relativism, with the result that our children have been losing a clear understanding of the very principle of right and wrong. If we return to the Ten Commandments, we will begin to build again on more wholesome and enduring foundations.

The God who reveals himself

The Ten Commandments begin with the thunder of direct revelation: 'I am the Lord your God.' What is presented is not the possibility of the divine, but the fact of a God who is self-revealed. This revelation is focused on a specific event, the miraculous liberation of the Jews from Egypt, when a weakened slave race were able to secure their freedom as a result of a whole series of extraordinary events that they readily understood to be the direct interventions of God on their behalf. The Jewish understanding is therefore not simply that any page of human history demonstrates the reality of God, but rather that God reveals himself in specific interventions, mysterious events that demonstrate the divine character and power in action. For the Jew, the revelation of God in history is found supremely in the Old Testament in the great liberation of the Jews from Egypt. This became the defining moment for the sense of national identity as the people of God. Their first, historic liberation has remained the type and inspiration for their continuing expectation of liberation from every tyrannous overlord in the succeeding centuries. The God who liberated always remains true to his character and so will liberate again. The dogged persistence of Jewish identity across the many centuries of persecution and marginalisation, finds its inspiration in the ultimate dependability of their Liberator God.

For Christians, the revelation of God in the Jewish Exodus continues to be cherished, but the ultimate revelation of God in history is found in Jesus Christ, his incarnation, death and resurrection. The existence of Jesus as a real person in history is subject to historical analysis. The resurrection of Jesus is not merely a statement of faith, but the evidence can be explored. But beyond the history is the One revealed by these acts of liberation. The historical events point beyond themselves and can only find an

adequate explanation in the reality of the God who inter-
venes, revealing himself on the pages of human history.
The historical events are not only subject to objective
examination, but they also need to be explained, and for
Jews and Christians alike the only adequate explanation is
found in the God of history, whose actions reveal not only
his existence but his character, and the demands he makes
upon all who accept that he is indeed the God who is there.

Pointers towards God

Biblical morality, grounded in the Ten Commandments,
begins not with the human condition but with God, just as
biblical theology begins not with the concept of God, but
with the revelatory events of biblical history. This is an
alien way of thinking about religion in the modern world.
Talk about God is likely to provoke one of two responses,
and both are frequently dismissive. Some say, 'But I don't
believe there is a God.' Others explain, 'But I'm just not
religious.'

It is perfectly possible to construct a set of arguments for
the existence of God, and this has been an endeavour of
philosophical theology over many centuries. There is an
argument from design – the orderliness and beauty of
creation point to a designer and not to the random chaos
of spontaneous, chance events. There is an argument from
cause and effect – every action has a source, leading us back
to the ultimate source, that is God. There is an argument
from morality – the prevailing sense of right and wrong in
different cultures, despite the fact that some may be can-
nibals and others polygamous, points to an ultimate source
of moral values, since no adequate explanation of morality
can be derived from the animal world. There is an argument from spirituality – every human society has a religious
dimension, in quest of God, and primitive societies generally express a belief not only in the many gods of animism,

but behind these minor divinities they speak of the One High Unseen God. Some kind of awareness of the divine seems integral to the human condition. Philosophers debate the validity and force of these various arguments. Some have held that the traditional Western arguments for the existence of God are so conclusive that only a knave or fool could fail to be persuaded by them. Others have sought to reverse the force of these arguments, thus claiming that the classic so-called proofs are actually disproofs of the existence of God.

Several centuries ago, the great French thinker, Blaise Pascal, described the focus of these debates as the 'god of the philosophers'. Pascal noted an underlying problem, for if my faith in God is constructed upon these arguments, then my faith is dependent on my remembering the arguments. If I forget the arguments, I lose faith in the God to whom they point. We might add that if God's existence was indeed dependent upon my grasp of philosophical argumentation, my faith would daily be subject to the possibility of repudiation, since it would need to be suspended whenever I lost an argument with an atheist who was more adept at philosophical dispute.

There was a time when people thought they could finally prove or disprove the existence of God by utilising philosophical arguments. Now it is generally accepted that such arguments can at best do no more than suggest the possibility of God. They are pointers, not proofs. But Pascal's most important observation concerns the results of such discussion. Whether the arguments are utilised to prove or point towards the existence of a god, no specific notion of God can be proposed on this basis alone. These philosophical debates are about the possibilities of divinity, and there is a huge jump from the abstract concept of divine existence to the specific qualities and living reality of an actual God whom we can know and worship, love and serve. Someone may be able to rehearse every argument for the existence of God and be convinced of God's existence without it making a shred of difference to how they live. The god of the philosophers is constrained to be substantially less than the God of the Bible, who reveals himself in historical particularity. The Bible is consistently silent about arguments for God's existence. They are not repudiated as worthless, but they are never presented as the necessary preparation for faith. Biblical faith is first historical, presenting a God who gets his hands dirty in the specifics of human history as he works to bring liberation to his creation.

Jesus: God in history

For the Christian, the historical dimension of the first commandment – 'I am the Lord your God who brought you out of Egypt' – finds its ultimate expression in the historicity of Jesus Christ and his resurrection. Jesus is referred to outside the New Testament by Roman historians – in Tacitus directly and in Suetonius indirectly. The great Jewish historian, Josephus, also had no difficulty in acknowledging the fact that Jesus was a real person on the pages of human history:

> Now there was about this time, Jesus, a wise man, if it is lawful to call him a man, for he was a doer of wonderful works – a teacher of such men as receive the truth with pleasure. He drew over to him both many of the Jews and many of the Gentiles. He was Christ; and when Pilate, at the suggestion of the principal men among us, had condemned him to the cross, those that loved him at first did not forsake him, for he appeared to them alive again on the third day, as the divine prophets had foretold these and ten thousand other wonderful things about him; and the tribe of Christians, so named after him, are not extinct at this day.

As to the New Testament documents, comparisons with other writings from antiquity bear striking results. Nine or ten early copies of Caesar's *Gallic War* still survive, the oldest coming from around 900 years after Caesar's death. Twenty copies of Livy's Roman history are available, and again the intervening period is around 900 years. Only eight copies of Herodotus' writings survive, and the interval is 1,300 years. In the centuries since the invention of the printing press, such time gaps may seem enormous and yet no classical scholar would doubt the authenticity of these manuscripts.

In the case of the New Testament, the earliest full manuscript of the complete New Testament dates from around AD 350. There are in addition manuscripts of individual New Testament books and fragments, 5,000 Greek manuscripts, 10,000 Latin manuscripts, and 9,300 others. The earliest writings can be confidently dated to within a few years of the death of Jesus, that is within the lifetime of the generation of eyewitnesses. In addition, there are 36,000 citings of the New Testament in the writings of the early church fathers from the first four centuries of Christianity. In short, the sheer enormity of the data and the tiny interval between the earliest surviving manuscripts, the date of original composition, and the events of Jesus' own lifetime all combine to provide the highest degree of certitude. It is beyond all reasonable doubt in the eyes of any serious historian that Jesus of Nazareth was a genuinely historical figure.

Resurrection and history

The conclusion that the historicity of the person of Jesus is beyond dispute does not require faith in him or adherence to his teachings. What it does indicate is that the Christian faith, like Judaism, is rooted in events that are both historical and extraordinary. For Christians, however, the pivotal issue concerning Jesus is not merely that he existed, but that he was raised from the dead. Once more the evidence is considerable and readily examined.

The first factor is the empty tomb. All the New Testament accounts agree that when some of the believers visited the tomb where Jesus' body had been laid, the burial chamber was no longer occupied. It was in the same city of Jerusalem that the resurrection of Christ was first preached, and such talk would have made the first Christians the laughing stock of Jerusalem if the tomb still contained a body, since what was proclaimed was not the continuation of Jesus' spiritual ideals, but the historical miracle of his bodily resurrection. If those hearing the message had visited the tomb of Jesus and found it still occupied, the Christian message would have expired within days of its first proclamation.

Given that the tomb was empty, someone might have stolen the body. The Jewish and Roman authorities sealed up the tomb and set a guard outside, presumably because they wanted to make sure Jesus' followers did not try to steal the body. But if the disciples had stolen the body, and then made up the whole story of the resurrection, it seems inconceivable that not one of them should have confessed the hoax, since such proclamation hardly brought personal advantage. By preaching the historical resurrection, the first Christians faced persecution, imprisonment and martyrdom.

What if the authorities, having set a guard, then decided to remove the body for safe-keeping elsewhere? Quite simply, if they were responsible they could have destroyed the Christians' teaching overnight by exhibiting the decaying corpse in public and by announcing in public the confession of those paid to rob the grave. They were silent because they had no idea where the body had gone.

The second key factor is the resurrection appearances. Paul wrote to the Corinthians providing a long list of those who had seen Jesus in his resurrection (1 Cor 15:5–8).

Some had personal encounters, while the largest crowd that Paul reports contained some 500 people. Paul clearly presents these events as objective moments of recent history, since he explains that some of the eyewitnesses have died by the time he writes, but most are still alive. This represents a confident invitation to the Corinthians to check out the witnesses for themselves if they so desire. The appearances took place at different times, in different locations, with different groups of people. This rules out the possibilities of mass hysteria, whether spontaneous or deviously manipulated, since such fantasies of the imagination require a single location and a constant core group of participants.

Still more striking are two details of the resurrection narratives that set the first disciples in a poor light. First, they were surprised at the thought that Jesus had overcome death. This is hardly the kind of detail that would be included if the disciples were cooking up a hoax for personal gain. Second, the earliest eyewitnesses were women, and the first reaction of the male disciples was to dismiss their enthusiastic words as female excitability. Again, the reaction is not only sexist but also serves to make the men look foolish, since they subsequently come to agree with the women's celebration of Jesus' triumph over death. What's more, women were not accepted as reliable witnesses, neither in the world of the Roman Empire nor in contemporary Judaism. To begin the narratives of the resurrection with the witness of women was sheer stupidity if the intention was to invite others to believe, unless of course the women really were the first historical eyewitnesses to the resurrection of Jesus.

The third key factor is that lives were transformed. When Jesus was taken to be crucified, his closest friends were traumatised. Despite his clear teaching on the way to Jerusalem concerning his impending death, it had plainly remained inconceivable to them that such a prospect was imminent (Mk 8:31; 9:31; 10:33–34). In a state of shock and bewilderment, Peter denied Jesus three times, just as his master had predicted (Mk 14:66–72). Mark's Gospel adds the detail that one young man, quite possibly Mark himself, was only wearing a simple towel in the heat of the evening on the night of Jesus' arrest, and when the soldiers made a grab for him he dashed away naked into the night (Mk 14:51–52). In short, Jesus' followers were devastated by his arrest and execution, with neither a message to proclaim nor the courage to declare it.

After the resurrection, these same men were utterly changed. Their conviction that God had raised Jesus from the dead was unshakable. Their resolve to declare publicly the most astonishing event and person of human history was immovable. Nothing could silence them – neither threats from the authorities, who demanded that they keep this new religion to themselves, nor being roughed up and imprisoned, nor the fact that almost all the first-generation leaders ended their days as martyrs, executed for the truth that they proclaimed and by which they lived. The only reasonable explanation for this transformation is that the resurrection they proclaimed really had happened.

The fourth key factor is the practices of the early church. The first Christians were all Jews, and the formidable sense of Jewish identity is seen throughout the world today. The keeping of the Sabbath, taught in the fourth commandment, has characterised Jewish communities across the centuries. To secular Westerners, setting a day apart from the general pattern of life has become a luxury that many say we cannot afford. But for the Jews, the Sabbath has always been an intrinsic part of their lifestyle, their faith and their national identity. For the first Christians, therefore, it was nothing less than a cultural revolution to abandon the holy day of their nation. To set Sunday above Saturday was a change that was radical and profound. The reason was the resurrection: Sunday had become the Lord's Day, the day of release from the grave and therefore the natural focal point for Christian celebration in worship.

The centrality of the conviction that Jesus had been raised from the dead is just as evident in both the Lord's Supper and baptism. In the breaking of bread, the first Christians not only conducted a remembrance of Christ's crucifixion, but also a celebration of his present lordship and an anticipation of his return in glory (1 Cor 11:26). Likewise, in baptism, the believer who was immersed in water was understood to be symbolising a dying into the power of the cross of Christ. When the believer arose out of the water, that was understood to symbolise being raised into newness of life in the resurrection of Christ (Rom 6:3–4). The death of Christ was not an object of shame or regret to the first Christians, because they were confident that it was followed, as a definite event in human history, by the resurrection. The centrality of the cross and the resurrection together provide the pivotal theme of early Christian worship, the foundational tenet of faith.

The God who speaks

Such confidence in the God who reveals himself in human history is taken a step further both within the first commandment and throughout the Bible. Not only are the reality and the character of God revealed in specific interventions in human history, which can then be openly examined by future generations, but the same God also provides verbal revelation. That is, the inspired writings of the Old and New Testaments not only report the historical acts of God, but in themselves they are a further means of revelation. This is seen in the very wording of the Ten Commandments, for they are presented not merely as Moses' ethical reflections in the light of the miraculous Exodus, but rather as the very words of God.

This is not the appropriate book in which to explore models of biblical inspiration, but Christians continue to recognise the supreme authority of the Scriptures above the wisdom of any other writings and the traditions of the church, for in the Scriptures alone we believe that God has spoken with a definitive and enduring authority. The historical revelation of God is thus twofold: in his works and in his words. Moreover, the words continue to speak, for through them new faith continues to be kindled, our understanding of God continues to develop, and new encounters with God are brought about. The supreme status of the Scriptures does not preclude the possibility of personal experience of God, but all such intuitive encounters are interpreted by the unchanging revelation of the Scriptures. Nor does scriptural authority diminish the unique status of Jesus Christ – he is the Word of God made flesh, and the Scriptures reveal and interpret his life and teaching.

Only one God

There is therefore, in the very first of the commandments, an unapologetic and express absolutism. The God who speaks claims a unique authority both for himself and for his words. Without apology or hesitation, the God of the Bible is emphatically monotheistic: there is only one God and I am he. If this were a human conclusion or proposition, it would need to take its stand in the market-place of ideas, competing with other philosophies and perspectives. But the claim of the Bible is that the God of history is the God who speaks, and his works and words invite a categorical conclusion: this is your God, there is none other.

In a pluralistic society, Christians should be champions of respect for others and defenders of free speech against the intolerant, but at the same time Christians need to provide an unapologetic proclamation of the God of revelation in history and in Scripture, whose works are supremely seen in the Exodus of the Jews and the life, death and resurrection of Jesus Christ and whose words are found in the books of the Bible: 'And God spoke all these words. . . .'

2

You shall not make for yourself an idol
in the form of anything in heaven above
or on the earth beneath
or in the waters below.
You shall not bow down to them
or worship them;
for I, the Lord your God,
am a jealous God,
punishing the children
for the sin of the fathers
to the third and fourth generation
of those who hate me,
but showing love to a thousand
generations of those who love me
and keep my commandments.

Deuteronomy 5:8–10

The Second Commandment
No Place for Idols

Whenever we enjoy magnificent scenery or take pleasure in a concert, be it pop, rock or classical, most of us share the same impulse: we want to tell others about it. It's not simply that we want to tell them what they have missed; we also like to reminisce with others who have been to the same place or enjoyed a similar concert. The enjoyment is recaptured in telling others about it. The pleasure principle, the capacity to lose ourselves in appreciation of natural beauty or human artistry, is closely related to the worship principle, the desire to express our enthusiasms with a sense of wonder and even gratefulness.

Both pleasure and worship are integral dimensions of human existence. We are not only capable of moments of great enjoyment, but we also enjoy sharing with others these high peaks of life that transcend the world of the everyday. Worship is an extension of this instinctive desire to express deep appreciation. Expressing thanks to the Ultimate Giver of our pleasures neither diminishes us nor the pleasure itself. On the contrary, our lives and our pleasures are enhanced when we learn to give ourselves in worship.

No compromise

The second commandment recognises this innate tendency to express worship, by restricting the objects of such worship: all idols are excluded. So why is the Bible so consistently opposed to idols? The simplest answer lies in the strict monotheism of the first commandment. Following such an explicit claim that there is only one God, the legitimacy and validity of idol worship are expressly denied. Ancient Israel's history in the Old Testament represents a continued tension between those who seek comfort and security in idols and those who are prepared to hold to the exclusivities of a monotheism that excludes graphical representations of God. The best of the ancient Jewish kings joined with the prophets in this struggle for monotheistic purity, but many other kings of Israel and Judah were only too ready to assimilate their religion to the polytheistic consensus of the ancient Middle East.

The folly of idols

The exclusion of idols is logically twofold: both the physical representations themselves and equally any worship directed to the deities represented by such carvings, statues and ornaments. The Old Testament contains several uncompromising polemics that repudiate any possible legitimacy for idols and idol worship in Israel. Isaiah's invective is particularly emphatic:

The blacksmith takes a tool
  and works with it in the coals;
he shapes an idol with hammers,
  he forges it with the might of his arm.
He gets hungry and loses his strength;
  he drinks no water and grows faint.
The carpenter measures with a line
  and makes an outline with a marker;
he roughs it out with chisels
  and marks it with compasses.
He shapes it in the form of man,
  of man in all his glory,

that it may dwell in a shrine.
He cut down cedars,
  or perhaps took a cypress or oak.
He let it grow among the trees of the forest,
  or planted a pine, and the rain made it grow.
It is man's fuel for burning;
  some of it he takes and warms himself,
  he kindles a fire and bakes bread.
But he also fashions a god and worships it;
  he makes an idol and bows down to it.
Half of the wood he burns in the fire;
  over it he prepares his meal,
  he roasts his meat and eats his fill.
He also warms himself and says,
  'Ah! I am warm; I see the fire.'
From the rest he makes a god, his idol;
  he bows down to it and worships.
He prays to it and says,
  'Save me; you are my god.'
They know nothing, they understand nothing;
  their eyes are plastered over so that they cannot see,
  and their minds closed so that they cannot understand.
No-one stops to think,
  no-one has the knowledge or understanding to say,
'Half of it I used for fuel;
  I even baked bread over its coals,
  I roasted meat and I ate.
Shall I make a detestable thing from what is left?
  Shall I bow down to a block of wood?'

(Is 44:12–19)

Idols are intrinsically absurd, since the idol that is venerated as an object of spiritual power is no more than a work of human hands. They are also theologically inept, since the use of idols requires assent to three key assumptions. First, that it is conceivable for transcendent spiritual beings to be represented adequately by human artistry. Second, that it is possible to reduce a genuine god to the status of a household deity, domesticating supernatural power so that the little god is obliged by the idol that represents it to bring blessing upon a particular home. Third, that the power of such a god can then be directed, not only in blessing but even to bring a curse upon those hated by the idol worshippers.

Idols therefore face a double critique. The iconographic problem with them is that they represent the unrepresentable: it is the very nature of God's infinite transcendence that he is beyond graphical representation. Any attempt to portray God diminishes his infinite transcendence, confining his awesome otherness within the boundaries of human comprehension and artistry. However much graven images might seek to honour the God of Israel, they inevitably serve to distort and diminish his grandeur and glory. The aim of this restriction was not to exclude the representational arts from Israel, but rather to set this single limit on their subject matter: the living God is beyond representation by any artist, and so such attempts were forbidden.

At the same time, the manufacture and worship of idols demonstrate the human lust for power. Even as we are stirred to worship by experiences of great pleasure and beauty, we are tempted to resort to idols. They not only misrepresent God, but they also express the false hope that supernatural power can be tamed and harnessed for good and for ill, with little gods obliged to bring a blessing or curse on the targets of the prayers and rituals of the devotees. All too often, the instincts of worship are distorted by a craving for power, both power to command the little gods and power over and even against other people. Craven subservience to idols in the late twentieth century continues to be seen in many parts of the world, not only in the authority of tribal witch-doctors, but also in the anxiety-driven street corner offerings to idols still prominent in many large, highly developed South American cities.

Ancient idols

Modern pluralistic values emphasise the need to respect and give place to every expression of spirituality, giving more or less equal place and validity to every religion. It is therefore salutary to recall the characteristics of the particular idols confronted by ancient Israel. Baal was the most important of the Canaanite gods. His name means master, possessor or husband, and he represented the principle of domination and forcefulness, often portrayed as a storm god, brandishing thunderbolts. He was understood to be the ruler of other gods, dominant over death and infertility. For many centuries there was a continuing rivalry in Israel between those who considered Baal pre-eminent and those who served Jahweh (the LORD) alone.

Not only did the Canaanites worship many gods, but their gods were polygamous. One of Baal's most important consorts was Asherah, a mother goddess of fertility. Images of Asherah, known as Asherah poles, were very common in ancient Israel. As in many primitive fertility cults, her devotees not only worshipped the goddess of the cycles of nature, but also used the natural cycle as a basis or pretext for lasciviousness and a free and easy approach towards casual or ritual sex. The Israelites were under obligation to cut down or burn the Canaanite poles (Deut 12:3) and were forbidden to erect such poles beside their altars (Deut 16:21). Nonetheless, the attractions of a fertility cult, superstitions about the natural cycle or even an ill-conceived desire to provide a partner for Jahweh, led to a profusion of such fertility poles under many of the kings of Israel and Judah, much to the indignation of the Israelite prophets and historians.

Molech was a god of the Ammonites, and his worship entailed sacrificing children by throwing them into a fire. Such appalling barbarism was explicitly condemned by Moses' law, which expressly stated that anyone committing such an act should be condemned to death (Lev 18:21; 20:2–5). Nevertheless, Solomon built an altar to Molech on the Mount of Olives, outside Jerusalem (1 Kings 11:7) and two later kings, Ahaz and Manasseh, offered up their children as burnt sacrifices (2 Chron 28:3; 2 Kings 21:6). King Josiah destroyed the high places of Molech (2 Kings 23:10,13), but Ezekiel still needed to condemn the worship of Molech in the early sixth century BC (16:20ff; 20:26, 31; 23:37). The worship of Molech continued in North Africa into the early Christian era.

In addition to these deities of domination, sexual licence and child sacrifice, ancient Israel was also attracted by the twin deities of Fortune and Destiny (Is 65:11–12). These idols promised the vain hope of either discovering hidden knowledge about the future or even the possibility of controlling the future. Closely related to such hidden knowledge was the attraction of conjuring up the spirits of the dead and also astrology. Highly popular in the ancient world, such religious practices were expressly forbidden in Israel.

> Do not turn to mediums or seek out spiritists, for you will be defiled by them. I am the Lord your God (Lev 19:31).

> When men tell you to consult mediums and spiritists, who whisper and mutter, should not a people enquire of their God? Why consult the dead on behalf of the living? (Is 8:19).

> And when you look up to the sky and see the sun, the moon and the stars – all the heavenly array – do not be enticed into bowing down to them and worshipping things the Lord your God has apportioned to all the nations under heaven (Deut 4:19).

The common thread in these various forms of idol worship is more than an assault on the strict monotheism of Israel. In each case there is a concern with power, either to appease the power of a capricious and potentially dangerous spiritual force, or to direct that power either for personal gain, through blessing and the unmasking of secret and hidden – that is, occult – knowledge, or for the direct cursing of one's enemies. With such a worldview, men and women are almost obliged to live in a bondage of superstitious fear, victims of the idols they have set up. Modern liberal notions of tolerance tend to romanticise the religious practices of past generations. The Bible records the strenuous effort, across many centuries, to rid Israel of a seething mass of superstitions that were misguided, cruel and lascivious, deceitful, malevolent and frequently corrupting.

Virgil's *Aeneid* provides revealing insights into the superstitions of the Roman Empire. Human history is understood to be shaped not so much by human decisions or an inherent moral framework, but rather by the whims of a capricious pantheon of gods whose dealings with men and women are often casual, impulsive, lecherous and arbitrary. It is therefore hardly surprising that the early Christians were sometimes accused of atheism by the leaders of the Roman Empire. In a world of enslavement to idols, the 'people of the way', as the Christians first called themselves, demonstrated a strange and sometimes shocking freedom. Their confidence in the living God and their repudiation of all idol worship led them to a healthy and thoroughgoing disregard for the many gods, superstitions and anxieties of Roman religion.

Modern idolatry

Has the modern world escaped once and for all from the pantheon of ancient gods? Less has changed than we might have expected in the days when secular rationalism was at its height. Freemasonry continues to be prevalent, despite the many press reports that have suggested that the organisation is rife with corruption. Some senior officers have stated publicly their conviction that Freemasonry is an unhealthy pastime for any members of the police force, since it may compromise their credibility as totally impartial in their law enforcement. Within the Christian church, every denominational report on Freemasonry has concluded that it entails religious practices and convictions that are inherently incompatible with the Christian faith.

First, Freemasonry is syncretistic in its worship and prayers. This is demonstrated, for example, in the revelation to initiates of higher levels of a secret, masonic name of god, that is Jabulon, which is a compound of Jahweh, the God of the Bible; Baal, the idol against whose followers Elijah took a decisive stand in ancient Israel; and Osiris – On is a recognised abbreviation for the name of the Egyptian God. In June 1985, the Grand Secretary of Freemasonry, who holds high office in the Royal Arc, denied in an interview for Radio 4 the syncretistic implications of this name, explaining it away as merely representing inaccurate scholarship. However, when pressed he declined even to use the name on air, explaining that it was as unspeakable for him as the name of God was for the Jews. This clearly implied that the name was integral, indeed foundational, to the religion of Freemasonry.

The second great objection to Freemasonry as a legitimate social activity for any Christian believer is that it denies the necessity of the cross of Christ. Freemasonry has borrowed a number of traditional Christian prayers, but consistently removes from them any reference to the mediation of Christ.

The third great objection is that Freemasonry reinstates works as the basis of salvation, contradicting the fundamental New Testament principle of justification by faith: 'For it is by grace you have been saved, through faith – and this not from yourselves, it is the gift of God – not by works, so that no-one can boast' (Eph 2:8–9).

A few years ago, astrology was sneered at by many,

marginalised in the back pages of women's magazines. Now many high audience TV programmes, including the National Lottery show, have their resident astrologers. Lady Luck or Dame Fortune has made a comeback, gathering a new, devoted following among those who search for hidden knowledge in the stars. At the same time, long-standing patterns of idolatry, such as voodoo, have been joined by a resurgence of interest in witchcraft, Druidism and other ancient fertility religions. In many fashionable Western homes, crystals have become the new household gods, arranged to manage and direct spiritual forces towards the well-being of their owners. In the United States, Nancy Reagan consulted an astrologer from the White House, while Hillary Clinton has allegedly made use of a New Age medium. In Britain, the royal family has reportedly succumbed not only to wholesale sexual immorality and divorce, but also to New Age idolatry, with Diana, Sarah and Andrew all reputed to have consulted various gurus of crystals, stars and aromas. The ancient idols are enjoying a renewed allure at the end of the twentieth century.

Goods as gods

In a less obvious renewal of ancient idolatry, modern shopping malls can be looked upon as the great temples of secular consumerism. Many old town centres have been stripped of their main retail outlets as the larger shopping chains clamour for prime sites in the new malls. Like an ancient temple or a medieval cathedral, a modern mall is an enormous building with an imposing façade, dwarfing the homes of the devotees of the cult. Mood music and decor set a tone of well-being: the consumer must experience enough of the 'feel-good factor' to be prepared to part with their money, but not enough to feel satisfied without making new purchases. Broad walkways lead the devotees of the cult through the great building towards the high altar, the department store with the prime site at the top end of the building.

Shopping has become in the West the pre-eminent leisure pursuit of the middle classes. We worship at the altars of consumerism, buying goods that we don't need with money that we don't have. Many people explain that they buy things at the malls not because they need to, but to make themselves feel better. Shopping is no longer a wearisome duty, but a quasi-religious pursuit of meaning and happiness, identity and fulfilment. The Enlightenment defined human existence in terms of rationality – to think is to be. Existentialism looked to self-authentication through action – to do is to be. But in the modern West, a new mode of existence has been created – to shop is to be.

The price of idols

The worship of idols invariably has a price tag. For the old idols, resurgent in modern superstitions and neo-paganism, the price tag is control. The idols are about controlling life, placating the deities or discovering hidden knowledge. But the reality is that the idol worshipper becomes controlled by the idols – they offer the illusion of mastery over life, but in practice the devotee is mastered by the idol. Those who have sought power become ever more dependent upon the divinity and its priests, and the required religious practices. Readers of astrological charts and users of tarot cards tend to develop an ever greater, often compulsive dependence upon the sources of their hidden knowledge. The old Mephistophelean deal still holds: the price of seeking power and freedom among the false gods is ultimately the liberty of the human soul.

As for the new idols, those who live to shop must constantly return to the shopping malls. Material prosperity offers the illusion of fulfilment in the next purchase. But there is always something more to buy, a newer model with a higher specification. Once again, the devotee has the illusion of achieving control over life and the guarantee of lasting satisfaction. But the reality is constantly disappointed hopes, and a renewed need to come back and shop again. A generation ago, the West was getting used to the principle of built-in obsolescence, when consumer goods could be more or less guaranteed to expire after a limited number of years. Now we have entered a new age, where the replacements for high-tech goods are already being manufactured when the present model is still on sale in the shops at full price. Anyone who has bought a computer in the last five years has experienced this unpleasant sense of helpless frustration: six months after the purchase, the next model is much faster *and* cheaper as well!

Although the malls spend a great deal on creating a feel-good factor, they not only tear the heart out of town centres, but they are also indifferent to the traditional ideal of creating and sustaining a local community. An old town centre will often contain a market square or some other pleasant open space, where people can sit to rest, eat and meet friends, without any immediate pressure to make more purchases. At first sight, modern shopping malls have retained this concern to support community life, with the provision of seating often set around plants and fountains. However, the malls have learned from the fast food chains, where careful research has gone into providing seating that helps maximise turnover. In contrast to the unhurried atmosphere of a traditional restaurant, fast food outlets are not only designed to serve the customer without delay, but also to encourage the customer to finish their meal and leave the premises as quickly as possible, to make space for another sitting. In the same way, while the seating in a mall looks pleasant enough, it is never particularly comfortable. In fact it is typically a rudimentary bench with no back support. The reason is simple: time spent resting or talking with friends is time lost from shopping. The illusion is that the customer matters most, but in reality we matter considerably less once we have parted with our money. Everything is driven by the bottom line, with the result that investing in community enrichment has been deemed a luxury that the shopping malls cannot afford. That's why many complain that the malls are so impersonal. In pursuit of maximum profits, the malls have a much narrower and more sharply focused intention than an old town centre. They promote the pursuit of individualised, essentially isolated consumerism, at the expense of community life.

The sins of the fathers

In an age of counselling and psychotherapy, the biblical warning about the sins of the fathers being visited upon the children has been given new pertinence. The specific implications in this particular context are however much broader than the consequences of deficient parenting. George Eliot's novels are shaped by the 'doctrine of consequences', the conviction she developed that there is a moral order intrinsic to human life. Like the physical laws of cause and effect, when we contravene that moral framework there is a resultant rebound in our circumstances. Eliot recognised that these moral consequences are multiple, affecting both the 'sinner' and those 'sinned against'. In her secularised morality, Eliot was expressing a biblical conviction. The morality of the Ten Commandments should not be treated as a divine afterthought, a later bolt-on to the order of the cosmos. Rather, they express both the character of God and the moral order innate in creation and in human existence. When we abandon the commandments, we quickly begin to face the consequences, for we set in motion the creation of a hell on earth.

The ethical wisdom expressed in the commandments of

ancient Israel still holds good. When worship is directed rightly, it is life-enhancing, enriching our sense of self and the pleasures we enjoy. But when worship is directed wrongly, the eventual result, often unseen and imperceptible at first, is enslavement to destructive principles. Idol worship leaves men and women bound in chains of superstition and fear, compulsive habits, isolation and anxiety. The idols of materialism, New Age mysticism, astrology and occultism are as enslaving as the ancient idols of Baal, Asherah and Molech.

3

You shall not misuse
the name of the Lord your God,
for the Lord will not hold anyone guiltless who
misuses his name.

Deuteronomy 5:11

The Third Commandment
Misusing God's Name

Revising the blasphemy law

The British law on blasphemy has, in the eyes of many, fallen into disrepute. Prosecutions have been brought with extreme rarity, and so some ask whether this law has become unworkable. Others ask whether a specifically Christian blasphemy law is fair and reasonable in a modern, pluralistic society. While some defend an absolute freedom of speech that would entitle anyone to say anything about any god or faith, others suggest that the blasphemy law might be replaced with new legislation aimed at those who cause grievous religious offence or incite religious hatred.

This new approach would raise problems at least as great as the present law, as a result of a fundamental shift in emphasis from speaking detrimentally about a specific deity to provoking offence in the followers of any religion. How could such a subjective offence be measured, when some religions are decidedly less tolerant of opposition than others? Such a law could even make illegal any attempt to convert the adherents of another faith, since the witness might cause offence either to the person listening or to their co-religionists.

This is more than a theoretical possibility. In a number of Muslim countries today, if someone becomes a Christian they may escape with being excluded from their family, or they may even receive death threats. The very act of witness and evangelism has been shown to cause grievous religious offence and incite religious hatred. In July 1996 the case of Robert Hussein, a forty-seven-year-old Christian convert from Islam in Kuwait, was widely reported. Some Muslims had offered him large sums of money to recant, but he had refused. An Islamic court then ruled that he was guilty of apostasy, for which the punishment is death. Hussein spent the early summer fleeing from house to house, staying mainly with Western expatriates. He paid tribute to *The Times* for publicising his fate: 'It has been a miracle that I have survived for so long. Now many people have come forward to offer to help me because of your exposure of the terror I have lived with.' We therefore need to recognise that proposals intended to be liberal and generous in a multi-faith society could actually have the unfortunate result of severely restricting religious liberties, imposing a form of religious state censorship as repressive as that faced by the first Christian martyrs.

International blasphemy

The most notorious blasphemy case in recent years is of course the *fatwa* declared by the Ayatollah Khomeini against Salman Rushdie. For some Muslims, the offensiveness of Rushdie's novel, *The Satanic Verses*, was so great that the religious obligation to punish him was more important than the rule of international law. Anyone killing him would become a hero of the religion. The *fatwa* was nothing less than an incitement to international terrorism.

For Western cultural activists, the governing principle in the Rushdie affair has been quite different: the right to freedom of speech for the novelist. Irrespective of the degree of offence provoked by his novel, few non-Muslims are able to understand or accept the concept of a *fatwa*. If every religious grouping had the right to impose execution upon those who had blasphemed against their faith, the world would sink fast into anarchy. The rule of international law should be respected by all.

Blasphemy and art

Can there reasonably be a law on the statute books designed to protect God? More to the point, is such a law enforceable within a pluralistic society? There is much reason to doubt whether such a law is either workable or useful. *The Last Temptation of Christ* was a film that won short-lived notoriety by speculating about the supposed sexual fantasies of Jesus. For some, the film was a genuine work of art, asking original questions in a creative way. For others, it was a piece of cheap sensationalism, concerned like most Hollywood movies with making good box office sales. Ironically, the movie's profits could only be boosted by indignant Christian reactions. Its eventual showing on British television was met by a considerable outburst of public protest, but the blasphemy law could not keep it from the screens.

In a similar way, Monty Python's *The Life of Brian* actually gained notoriety and therefore larger audiences when Christians protested. Some Christians enjoyed the film, on the basis that Brian was not the genuine Messiah, but merely a very ordinary Galilean, stumbled upon by mistaken followers. They would probably have been rather more disconcerted by the subsequent revelation that the original title proposed for the film would have placed its offensiveness beyond all ambiguity: *The Life of Jesus*.

While some films claim to ask serious questions, whether or not the claim is credible, and others are obviously trivial, a third category of material is neither ambiguous nor attempting to be funny. One well-known American artist has displayed a crucifix suspended in a transparent box filled with urine. The title of the piece is the word 'Christ' preceded by a four-letter colloquialism for that particular liquid. This represents an aggressive, unapologetic and direct antipathy towards the Christian God. It is a telling indicator of a civilisation adrift from its roots that such militant and provocative anti-Christian iconography should be accepted as legitimate art in galleries of high renown. God is the ultimate judge of such enmity towards himself. The New Testament makes it plain that those who reject his love will not be obliged to endure his presence in eternity. . . .

Conversational cursing

It is not just modern art that has a problem with blasphemy. Everyday conversation is casually littered with the misuse of the name of God. In previous centuries, exotic neologisms made reference to Christ – 'Gadzooks' meant God's hooks, that is the nails that pinioned Jesus to the cross; 'Zounds' signified God's wounds; 'bloody' may well have referred originally to the blood of Christ. We may ask why it is so often Jesus Christ whose name is taken in vain, and not Gautama Buddha, Muhammad or Karl Marx. Does this simply reflect the Christian roots of our culture, and a casual repudiation of the dominant religion of the West? Does it reflect some kind of residual recognition that there is a distinctive spiritual authority in the name of Christ? Or does it simply recognise that while Christians may object to such swearing, they are on the whole unlikely to attempt to blow your brains out in retribution for such blasphemy? For many Christians, not least visitors from the developing world, the constant misuse of the name of Christ is indicative of a deep and pervasive antagonism to Christianity in the Western world.

In the latest Broadcasting Standards Council report of summer 1996, there was a greater number of complaints about programmes before the 9pm watershed that were concerned with bad language rather than with either sex or violence. By far the largest category was swearing with religious connotations, comprising 38% of the bad language monitored. Complaints were apparently received from both believers and unbelievers. Two of the main objections to bad language are as follows. First, the habitual and casual use of such language on television shows disrespect for the Christian faith and its adherents – it causes personal distress to many Christians to hear their God and Saviour's name evoked in such a way. Second, such language is subversive, an oblique attack on the faith, bringing the name of Christ into disrepute and further encouraging such debased use of his name by adults and children alike as something of no significance.

Caricatures of God

The name of God is also taken in vain by caricatures of what God is like. When a student called Simon announced that he didn't believe in God, I asked him what God he didn't believe in. He answered, 'A heavenly tyrant with a long white beard who imposes whatever he likes upon a helpless world.'

'Simon,' I was able to reply, 'I don't believe in that God either!'

Within the church, extremists of every hue provide their own caricatures of God. His name is taken in vain by hate-filled anti-communists who believe that the only good Russian is a dead Russian and that the most grievous sin is to be anti-American. His name is taken in vain by modernistic theologians who try to restrict God within their rationalistic world-view, a benign force for good incapable of any direct activity in the world, whether revelation, miracles or resurrection. His name is also taken in vain by those who, in seeking to defend the gospel of Christ, unchurch every Christian beyond their own narrow circle of unyielding conformity.

God and nationalism

One of the most common misuses of the name of God is when a nation attempts to monopolise all claim on God's favour, presuming a divine stamp of approval on national policy, especially in times of war. The kingdom of God embraces concerns far wider than the national interest. In the wars of Europe, national church leaders all too often went in for the sheer folly of constantly praying to God for victory for their nation, even as their enemies were praying for victory to the same God. The direct misuse of the name of God is found in any attempt to tie the God of all the earth to any narrowly nationalistic cause. During Mrs Thatcher's premiership, one of the most creditable acts of the leaders of the established church was to resist her call for a triumphalistic celebration of victory in the Falklands conflict.

A secondary misuse has frequently occurred in Britain, when Christian hymnbooks have included the song 'I vow to thee my country'. Here, the nation itself is divinised, when the devoted nationalist is invited to offer 'the love that asks no question'. There is nothing inherently wrong with patriotism. Indeed, whether cheering for the national team or enjoying the distinctives of national culture, patriotism can be both enjoyable and healthy, providing a sense of bonding within the national community. However, patriotism turns destructive when it is absolutised, whether in racial hatred or in the profoundly unChristian loyalty summed up in the old phrase: 'My country, right or wrong.' When the nation is divinised, it becomes an idol, and if God is then invoked to assist in the rule of Britannia, or any other nation state, then the name of God is surely taken in vain.

During the summer of 1996, the peace process in Northern Ireland became acutely brittle. When the RUC first stood in the way of the Protestant Orangemen who wanted to march through predominantly Catholic areas, the Orangemen interpreted such obstructiveness as symptomatic of a sellout by the British government to the nationalist cause. All they wanted to do was to honour their sense of history and national identity by marching the traditional routes. When the RUC changed their policy, and then removed the Catholics from their own streets to make way for the marchers, it was the Catholics' turn to be aggrieved. It seemed that the British government was never going to stand in the way of the demands of the Orangemen, no matter how much these marches restricted the civil liberties of Catholic communities. On both sides, as the language of confrontation became more heated, political leaders seemed to be playing into the hands of the forces of polarisation and violence. The stand-offs fuelled resentment and thus support for terrorism, both IRA and loyalist.

No one outside Northern Ireland can pretend to understand the historical and cultural complexities of this conflict, but two principles must surely be stated. First, the commitment to a particular set of religious convictions must be set within a recognition of the political reality that Catholics and Protestants, Republicans and Unionists are here to stay, and it's about time they began to learn to live together. Northern Ireland desperately needs the leadership of statesmen who will take a stand for peace and democracy, spelling out the vital need to honour and protect the minority population. Second, taking a stand for Christian convictions needs to be kept distinct from the specifics of any particular political or tribal grouping. Every Christian leader should emphatically denounce the use of violence on all sides. More than that, I am personally unable to comprehend how any Christian leader could with integrity take part in the Orange marches or fail to repudiate both the IRA and the Unionist terrorists. They blur the necessary line between faith and politics, faith and nationalism. The hatred and bigotry expressed by many self-styled Christians in Northern Ireland is a terrible blight upon the Christian gospel throughout the United Kingdom. All who claim the name of God for their cause alone reinforce the antipathies of Northern Ireland, and are surely in grave risk of taking in vain the name they claim to hold so dear.

For the first Christians, this commandment brought them into early conflict with the Roman Empire. The cult of turning emperors into gods was partly religious but largely a means of enforcing the authority of the empire. All inhabitants of the empire came under an obligation to make the confession, 'Caesar is Lord.' The Greek word for Lord, *Kyrios*, had been used in the official Greek translation of the Hebrew Scriptures for the name of God. Thus, the early Christian declaration 'Jesus is Lord' not only declared Christ's authority over the believer's life, it also represented a clear confession of his divinity as the only begotten Son of God. It was therefore quite impossible for the Christians to make the required confession concerning Caesar. To do so would have been a fundamental denial of their uncompromising monotheism and above all of their convictions about Jesus Christ. For the Roman authorities, this principled refusal led to two accusations. First, that the Christians were irreligious, since they repudiated the many gods of the empire; and second, that their faith made them fundamentally disloyal and subversive, setting the kingdom of God above the Caesars and their empire.

In an age when political leaders are no longer divinised in the West, the confession that Jesus is Lord still has a continuing and radical impact. Where absolute loyalty is given to Christ, the demands of nationalism are moderated and relativised, for we have chosen a higher devotion than patriotic fervour. The absolutism of Christ's lordship moderates every other claim to authority. Christians may still be patriotic and loyal citizens, but their first commitment is to Christ. We can no longer say, 'My country, right or wrong,' but rather, 'My country, so long as its priorities do not contradict or contravene my primary devotion to the lordship of Christ.'

Human respect and morality

Some may wonder why God should be so concerned to protect his own name in the third commandment. Does this suggest some kind of divine insecurity or defensiveness? A more helpful interpretation of this commandment recognises the interconnectedness of God and humanity, and also of God and morality. As to humanity, the Jewish and Christian understanding is that men and women are created in the image of God. Those who honour God must also show due respect to every human being, irrespective of race, gender, social status, abilities, money or power. All are made in the image of God, so that to mistreat any person is to show disrespect for God. Conversely, therefore, to show disregard for God leads to a diminished respect for our fellow human beings. The consummate failure of the Crusaders, the Conquistadors and the Spanish Inquisition to grasp this concept does not invalidate the principle. When we truly honour God, we will also learn to honour all who are made in his image, including those who decline to accept our faith.

The connection between God and morality is equally fundamental. The Ten Commandments present themselves as a revealed morality, not constructed by men and women, but delivered by divine inspiration. They claim to provide not a set of provisional suggestions or a law code specific to a single culture and generation, but rather a framework of moral absolutes. In the Western world at the end of the twentieth century, increasing concern is being expressed that our children seem no longer able to tell right from wrong. With every new set of statistics concerning rising crime among children and teenagers, social commentators frequently voice anxiety at an sense of imminent moral collapse. A civilisation founded upon Christian values that repudiates the Christian God, in a rising tide of militant atheism and casual misuse of the name of Jesus Christ, will inevitably lose its moral cohesiveness. There can only be absolute standards of behaviour if there is an absolute reference point. Absolutes of morality require an absolute deity. The collapse of morality and the final demise of our civilisation may have imperceptibly begun with the casual and habitual cursing and careless disregard for the name of the Judaeo-Christian God.

4

Observe the Sabbath day by keeping it holy, as
the Lord your God has commanded you.
Six days you shall labour
and do all your work,
but the seventh day is a Sabbath
to the Lord your God.
On it you shall not do any work,
neither you, nor your son or daughter,
nor your manservant or maidservant,
nor your ox, your donkey
or any of your animals,
nor the alien within your gates,
so that your manservant and maidservant may
rest, as you do.
Remember that you were slaves in Egypt
and that the Lord your God
brought you out of there
with a mighty hand and an
outstretched arm.
Therefore the Lord your God
has commanded you to observe the Sabbath day.

Deuteronomy 5:12–15

The Fourth Commandment
Keeping the Sabbath

When it comes to working long hours, Britain is out of line. The average working week in Europe is 40.3 hours, but in Britain we work 43.4 hours. In November 1993 the European Union agreed to set a maximum working week of forty-eight hours as a health and safety measure. In addition, the following provisions were agreed: rest breaks every six hours; a minimum daily rest period of eleven hours; no more than eight hours' work on average for night-shift workers; three weeks' holiday per year (four by 1999); and at least one day off per week. It was not designed to be a radical employment directive. As Barbara Nolan, spokesperson for the EU Social Affairs Commissioner, observed, 'It's a minimalist piece of legislation and most countries already have tougher laws.'

Britain abstained from that vote and the British government has continued to object to this kind of European legislation, arguing that it compromises national sovereignty and interferes with the right of individual workers to negotiate their own hours of employment. It's not that British workers are notably more productive than our European competitors, we just seem to be tied to our desks or workbenches for more hours every week. Modern technology and industrial decline in Britain have led to less available work, and therefore higher underlying levels of unemployment. It is one of the ironies of the last decade that those who have retained their jobs often find themselves working longer hours with every passing year. The intention is to work in order to live; the reality is that many find themselves living in order to work.

While other European countries are committed to improving standards at work, some fear that the future of Britain is being shaped by a misguided policy of attempting to compete head on with the low-cost economies of Asia. While the European Union looks to add new legislation to protect workers, the British government is committed to a policy of sustained deregulation. The liberalisation of Sunday trading has been a key factor in this process, clearing away as many restrictions as possible in order to create an increasingly *laissez-faire*, free-market economy.

Reasons for the Sabbath

The fourth commandment has two distinct but complementary emphases. First, it is a day to be kept *holy*, 'a Sabbath to the Lord your God' (Exod 20:10). This speaks of the importance of setting aside one day from the regular routines of work in order to devote quality time to worship. Just as emphatically, the day is set apart as a day of *rest*, and the commandment spells out that not only the privileged, but all people should be exempt from work one day a week: 'On it you shall not do any work, neither you, nor your son or daughter, nor your manservant or maidservant, nor your animals, nor the alien within your gates' (Exod 20:10). The Sabbath therefore not only provided an opportunity for worship, but also secured a breathing space from daily tasks for everyone in Israel.

The Sabbath has remained remarkably intact among orthodox Jews. Throughout the many centuries of Jewish history, Jews have preserved the distinctive character of a Jewish Saturday. In addition to worship and rest, the third great Jewish ingredient is of course time with the family, for the Sabbath also involves a celebratory meal in God's presence, enjoyed by the whole family together.

For the first Christians, despite their Jewish heritage, there was an early and decisive shift from Saturday to Sunday. This looks like a symbolic expression of grace: now we get to rest and worship not on the last day of the week but the first; not after a week's work but before the week has begun. The decisive factor, however, was not a theology of grace applied to the work-place, but the historical event of the resurrection. Since Christ first appeared on the Sunday following his crucifixion, this day became the 'Lord's Day', the most natural day on which to meet to worship, pray and share the Christian equivalent of the Passover meal – the Lord's Supper.

Arguments against deregulation

When practising Christians are a minority in the nation, to set aside a day specifically for Christian worship is generally seen to be an unwarranted intrusion and imposition, a religious luxury that the economy of the nation cannot afford. In the recent Sunday trading debates in Britain, the objections to deregulation were chiefly concerned with the second great principle of the fourth commandment: the need for weekly rest. Great disquiet was expressed by those whose lives would be involuntarily disrupted by a seven-day shopping week. First, shop-workers and also those who clean the streets and remove refuse would have to become available for work on Sundays. Second, those living near shopping centres and shoppers' car parks who would no longer have a day free from crowds and noise. Third, those who run corner shops to serve a local community were seen to be at risk of losing their business because of increased competition from the large stores. Fourth, those who rely most upon corner shops are those without private cars, usually the poor and the elderly, and they would be condemned to the role of helpless observers of a rapid deterioration in the availability and variety of local shops that would inevitably diminish their own quality of life. Fifth, family life was seen to be at risk. In many homes, Sunday is the only day when a whole family still eats together. With deregulation, those in paid employment may all have different days off, so there is no longer any time in the week securely set aside for the family. A day off midweek does little to help strengthen family life for anyone whose children attend school Monday to Friday.

Above all, the poor were seen to be vulnerable in the face of deregulation: retail workers are usually badly paid and rarely unionised effectively. The fear was voiced that these workers would be imposed upon in two ways. They would be made to work at inconvenient and unsociable times in order to suit the demands of the middle classes. They would also see the initial incentives whittled away, as Sunday working gradually moved from being seen as exceptional and therefore deserving higher rates of pay, until eventually Sunday would be a day to work on standard shifts, no different from any other working day.

Although the government faced a battle to get the legislation through parliament, it was determined and eventually succeeded. The levels of demand for Sunday trading have since indicated that this has been a resounding success. Sundays have become one of the most important days for many leading retailers, generating a high proportion of the weekly turnover. The retailers are happy, the customers are happy, and when the changes were first introduced the shop-workers generally declared themselves more than willing to earn higher rates of pay by working on Sundays. Can we therefore conclude that the Sabbath has become a dead issue, an obsolete commandment that must be consigned to gather dust as an ancient irrelevance?

Caught on the treadmill

Life is getting faster in the Western world. People are finding it more and more difficult to take time to relax. Children have been sucked into this culture of relentless achievement. There was a time when children would simply play together after school. Now middle-class parents rush them from a music class to a sports experience and then to a personal tutor, paying for a different organised activity every night of the week. We are turning our children into a generation of super-achievers, who can do so very much that they have almost forgotten how to be.

In the United States, many shops and entertainment centres are open 364 days a year. Some suggest that there is more to this than libertarian capitalism. We seem to be facing a crisis of identity: to be is to be busy. We define ourselves and our sense of self-worth through constant activity, achievement and acquisition. The driving need to maximise profits and improve on last year's figures is continually reinforcing this trend, marginalising any desire for rest as an unfortunate and uneconomic necessity. We are becoming a society open for business seven days a week, twenty-four hours a day. The Sabbath principle cries out against this relentless and frenetic pace. We need time to relax, time for relationships, time just to be.

Contracted to Sunday working

As a result of deregulation, contracts of employment are changing. Initially, people were asked whether they would be prepared to work the occasional Sunday in addition to their normal work. It was overtime at a high rate of pay. People in retailing have described to me a second phase, in which Sunday trading was still additional but treated as normative. During this period, candidates would be asked at interview, 'What is your attitude towards Sunday trading?' To the financial incentive of 'Think of the extra money you'll earn!' was added an obligation to colleagues: 'If you don't work your fair share of Sundays, you'll be letting the team down.' Emotional pressure was frequently added to financial reward in order to extract compliance, willing or reluctant, from the workforce.

A third phase has now arrived, which many anticipated before deregulation. New contracts in retailing tend no longer to specify which days will be worked, but simply state that the employee will 'work time as specified'. These mild-mannered words denote a fundamental shift: Sunday working is no longer an optional extra, but an integral and obligatory part of the working week. One retail manager from Sainsbury's stated, 'Willingness to work on Sundays will obviously be one, although clearly not the only, factor that we have to take into account when making appointments . . .' (*Independent*, 23 November 1993). Some retailers have gone further. While those employed in the days before Sunday trading continue to receive premium rates of pay for working on Sundays, new employees sign contracts which exclude these premiums. In other words, freedom of choice for workers is being eroded and the financial rewards are being reduced.

The shareholders of large retailers are sitting pretty, for Sunday trading has significantly boosted turnover and profitability for the large stores. The boarded-up windows and 'for sale' signs outside small retail outlets around the country tell the other side of the story – if consumers are spending more in the big stores, corner shops have an ever-smaller slice of the cake. Big is beautiful in retailing, and while the out-of-town shopping centres are booming, it's not just corner shops that are an endangered species. Many high streets are facing extinction too.

The right to rest

The Sabbath principle is much broader than the Sabbath practices of orthodox Jews, among whom an electric light cannot be turned on because that would constitute an act of labour. To the non-Jew, there is something not only legalistic but really quite absurd about such devices as a Sabbath lift in an Israeli hotel – a special lift without buttons that stops at every floor, so that the faithful can get to the floor of their choice without the trouble of using the stairs, but without actually *working* the lift.

In Jesus' day the Jewish understanding of the Sabbath, at least among the Pharisees, had become essentially and overwhelmingly negative. Concern for the day was expressed in the rigorous exclusion of all manner of daily activities. The Pharisees were eager to see whether Jesus would heal on the Sabbath, since this would prove conclusively that he could not be counted among the holy men. Jesus not only healed, he vigorously repudiated their negativity: 'The Sabbath was made for man, not man for the Sabbath' (Mk 2:27). In accordance with Jesus' perspective, we can therefore conclude that the Sabbath needs to be understood not as something imposed in order to constrict life, but rather as something provided in order to secure time for rest and time for family and friends, as well as an opportunity for worship.

Just as Sabbath lifts and other Sabbatarian paraphernalia are inconceivable in the modern Western world, there is also sure to be no return to the days when pubs and cafés, sports and leisure centres were shut. Everyone except the most rigid Sabbatarians would probably agree that the following categories of work and trading on Sundays are well worth retaining.

- *Recreational venues, including sports facilities and restaurants*, provide rewarding opportunities for social and family time.

- *Emergency services* cannot cease on any day.
- *Corner shops* supply emergency provisions of all kinds, as well as newspapers.
- *Transport links* are also vital in an era when families and friends are often scattered across the country.
- *Garden centres and DIY stores* provide the necessary resources for many leisure activities – and emergency repairs!

We do still need to ask whether large retail outlets should be allowed to open on Sundays. The general public have voted with their feet to demonstrate that they enjoy this extra day of shopping, but we are yet to face the hidden costs of our relentless consumerism. When we wake up to the death of the corner shop and the introduction of compulsory Sunday working, it may be too late to reverse the commercial and contractual pattern. There is a good deal more to life than work and shopping!

We also need to consider as a society whether we want to resist the present trend in which more and more companies outside of retailing begin to request and then gradually come to require regular Sunday working. Selfridges, a leading London department store, decided at first only to open on Sundays in the run-up to Christmas, but following what they called 'a successful trial' in July 1996 they announced that they would be open every Sunday until further notice. In the summer of 1996, libraries looked set to conform to the new pattern, with one of the reasons being pressure from local retailers who found that they did more business when the libraries were open. Market pressures will surely increase upon other industries and professions to follow the lead of retailing. In order to compete, they will have to keep up with the availability of their competitors, and that is increasingly likely to mean constant availability of staff, seven days a week.

For as long as the present development of Sunday trading continues, Christians in the West are living in a culture that is not shaped by the Christian Sabbath. This is no new thing, since the first Christians naturally did not enjoy the support of the Roman Empire in their conviction that every Sunday had become special as a result of the resurrection of Christ. Similarly, missionaries in the Muslim and Jewish, Hindu and Buddhist world must serve and worship in a society that does not recognise Sunday as a special day. Christians in the West therefore need to discover new ways of applying the incarnational principle of mission. Jesus and the apostles spent time where the people were, rather than rebuking them for not attending the synagogue or an early Christian gathering.

In the same way, Western Christians need to develop evangelism strategies for the shopping centres where Sunday trade is brisk, often on the doorstep of church buildings. Our message surely does not need to be one of immediate and unfriendly rebuke. Rather, we want to celebrate and demonstrate the vitality and richness of living faith in the Christ who is alive today. Instead of saying, 'You shouldn't be shopping!', we can declare with confidence, 'We've found something much better than sale prices or special offers – the free gift of abundant and eternal life in Jesus Christ!'

The fourth commandment expresses a human right that the European Union is also seeking to defend in recent employment legislation. No thinking Christian should ever countenance any attempt to make worship compulsory, as true worship can only be expressed out of a free, personal choice. But no Christian committed to biblical justice can ignore the cost to the weak and the poor of the *laissez-faire* deregulation of working hours. By preserving the Sabbath, we protect time for the family and we affirm the richness of life beyond material acquisitiveness. Many of the most important aspects of life, such as love, truth and beauty, can never be quantified on an accountant's balance sheet.

The Sabbath principle affirms and seeks to preserve three foundational components of what it means to be fully human that our society is in danger of forgetting: a right to rest; a right to protected, quality time for family and friends; and an opportunity for worship.

5

Honour your father and your mother,
as the Lord your God
has commanded you,
so that you may live long
and that it may go well with
you in the land
the Lord your God is giving you.

Deuteronomy 5:16

The Fifth Commandment
Honouring Parents

The focus of the commandments shifts with the fifth. The first three are God-centred, and the fourth is concerned with protecting the right of rest and the opportunity for worship. The fifth focuses upon family life, although its implications are readily extended into society in terms of showing respect to those in authority and to older generations.

A crisis in parenting

Parenting has become devalued in late-twentieth-century Western society. Middle-class couples are delaying having a family, so that an increasing number of first-time mothers are over thirty. There seems to be three main factors in this trend: the need to bring in two incomes in order to finance a mortgage; the concern of women to get properly established in a career before having children, in order to minimise the risk of missing out on future promotion when they return to work; and the desire of many in their twenties to have a good time, maximising the period in which growing disposable income can be spent on leisure – often including exotic holidays – before settling down to parental responsibilities. Some have identified this emerging trend as a 'second adolescence' being indulged among the generation in their twenties and early thirties who inhabit a Peter Pan world, living 'in the now', in a dizzying whirl of parties and pleasure, while deferring for as many years as possible final entry into one of the full obligations of adulthood. For some, children become an inconvenience, even an impediment in a culture driven by career and consumerism. Devotees of consumerism do have one further regrettable attitude to children. When they can finally be deferred no longer, designer babies have become in some circles the latest and ultimate fashion accessory, dressed to impress, as little living mannequins of conspicuous consumption.

The social value placed on parenting has diminished considerably. Those women – and in the vast majority of families it is the woman – who choose to spend time at home to bring up young children can often be heard to apologise for their role when asked what they do: 'I'm *just* a housewife.' The term 'home-maker' is much more affirmative, emphasising the role of building and sustaining the micro-community of the nuclear family rather than suggesting an exclusive responsibility for cleaning and cooking. The newer term has not gained much popularity, but defensive apologies are all too familiar on the lips of those fulfilling a role that is looked down upon as 'economically unproductive' and may even imply a personal surrender in the battle of the sexes. In part this reflects economism, in which every task is valued according to its economic productivity. 'What do you do?' has become a euphemism for 'How much are you worth?' The defensiveness also reflects an unfortunate side-effect of feminism. Thirty years ago, the social pressure dictated that a career woman who was also a mother was something of an oddity, at risk of letting down her children. Some went as far as to say that a career was *'unfeminine'*. The pressure to conform has now been reversed, so that it is the woman who chooses to stay at home who often feels instinctively guilty, as if withdrawing from the work-place is a betrayal of her sex. Today's implicit charge is that choosing not to work is '*un-feminist*'.

Parents who choose or are obliged to go out to work often have to battle with the conflicting priorities of work and home. When considering the Sabbath commandment, we noted that many people have found themselves working ever longer hours as the twentieth century draws to a close. Young children are often still asleep when their working parents leave the house in the morning, and they have gone to bed before the parents arrive home. Many parents try to make up for their frequent Monday to Friday unavailability by buying the latest consumer goodies. Twenty years ago British parents looked askance at the bedrooms of American children, but now our children's bedrooms are replete with televisions, computers and phones. The gifts are meant to be demonstrations of love, but they are poor substitutes for quality time and personal attention. Almost every child will at some time demand the latest expensive toy advertised on TV, often making a manipulative comparison with other families, 'All my friends have already got one!' Some parents are faced with a more profound complaint after their children have reached adulthood: 'Wherever were you when I needed you the most?'

There are further ironies in a constant supply of presents as a substitute for spending time with the children. The presents that are meant to express love begin to instil in many children a value system that rates things above relationships. We are turning our children into little materialists, more addicted to conspicuous consumption than any previous generation. Worse still, when our gifts turn a child's bedroom into a comprehensive collection of electronic goods, we are undermining the opportunities for family time spent relaxing together. The child almost inevitably withdraws from the community of the family into a private world, choosing their own entertainment in the privacy of their room. Our intentions are relational, but the consequences can so easily backfire. No one has ever suggested that parenthood would be easy. . . .

Generational divides

Teenagers did not exist as a distinct consumer group in society before the fifties. A new age of existence was invented somewhere between the innocence and dependency of childhood and adult responsibility, as more children stayed at school than in previous generations, freed from the need to go out to work as soon as they had the strength to earn their keep. The growing disposable income of the young, often unfettered by any need to pay for housing and food, has resulted in the rapid emergence of a distinctive and highly profitable teenage market in music, fashion and entertainment. As the baby boomers turn grey, the number of teenagers has declined, but they have established a clear niche in the economy and a distinct generational identity.

More recently a further generational identity has emerged. Thirty years ago, many people retired with an expectation of almost imminent death. Apart from the handful who enjoyed exceptional longevity, to retire meant to be 'past it', entering the home straight of human existence. Today there are two quite distinct generations beyond sixty. First there are *the active retired*, who reject the very suggestion that they are 'elderly' and often enjoy a vigorous life of sport and travel. Then there are the parents of that generation, the second generation beyond retirement, who are appropriately termed *the elderly*, slowing down in the last season of life.

With this growing number and diversification of generational identities, there is an increased prospect of intergenerational rivalry. Those in middle years may find themselves still providing for adolescents who have not yet embarked upon independent adulthood, and at the same time be faced with the need to provide support for their own parents or grandparents in the second generation of the retired. This complex of dependent relationships makes enormous and often conflicting demands on time, money and emotional energy. It can also create a crisis of identity among those caught in the middle, whose role has become so pivotal: to their teenage children they are considered beyond all doubt to be old fogeys, while to their elderly relatives they are still young whippersnappers.

Choosing to honour

The fifth commandment has a subtle inclusiveness, not restricting its applicability to young children in their parents' home. All generations are called upon to show honour and respect to their parents. The way that honour is expressed will change significantly in the different stages of life. Young children may simply obey, learning to do as they are told. Older children will show honour by listening to the reasons for a particular action commended by their parents. Teenagers will increasingly assert their own individuality, often making choices that do not conform to their parents' preferences, but the commandment calls them to continue to show respect, rather than trash their parents, ignore them, or storm out of rooms at regular intervals, slamming doors behind them. Adults will honour their aging parents, at first by respecting their continued independence and later by providing the necessary support as frailty sets in.

We need to emphasise the gender-inclusiveness of this commandment. This is a charter for neither patriarchy nor matriarchy, for mothers and fathers are deserving of equal honour. We should also note the clear implication of the commandment that the best environment in which to bring up children is a family. Neither communes, in which adults assume a collective parental authority, nor homosexual partnerships, to which children have been added artificially by adoption or surrogacy, are countenanced by the biblical commandment as an adequate alternative to the God-given combination of a mother and a father in the family home.

Between 1971 and 1991 the number of babies born outside marriage increased fourfold. By 1990 three out of ten births were outside marriage. As for births where the mother is under twenty, eight out of ten were outside marriage early this decade. In 1992, two million children were being raised in single-parent families. It is imperative to recognise that single-parent families arise from very different kinds of personal circumstance: death, divorce or illegitimacy. It is therefore profoundly unhelpful to lump all single-parent families together as a target of general disapproval. Since the biblical norm is that children are raised in the same home as their mum and dad, those attempting to fulfil the role of double parent are often in need of personal support and encouragement. The tasks of parenthood are enormously exacting.

Churches would do well to develop support structures, not only for parents within the congregation, but also to serve the wider local community. In an age when many complain that parenting is becoming ever more arduous, I suspect that many churches would generate a great deal of local interest, Christian and non-Christian, if they began to provide parenting classes and workshops with such themes as 'Preparing for Parenthood', 'Surviving the Early Years' and 'Help, There's a Teenager in My House!'.

Since Western society has been largely patriarchal, the commandment's deliberately balanced emphasis on both parents is striking. Just as men and women are equally made in the image of God, fathers and mothers are both due the same kind of respect. In some families, the children play the parents off against one another. In others, the parents compete for the child's favour, often rubbishing the rival parent. Henry James' *What Maisie Knew* is a brilliant and heart-rending exploration of this cruellest of rivalries. The broken fragments of the parents' relationship cut deeply into the heart of the child. Since the commandment bestows upon parents an equal honour, wise parents will be eager to foster respect for their partner in the heart of their child.

Undeserving parents

What of parents who have done little or nothing to win the respect of their children? Is the commandment universal or selective in its application? We have already noted that some parents have minimal rations of time for their children. Others are over-demanding, over-authoritarian or constantly negative. Still others inflict verbal, emotional and physical abuse. In 1991, over 31,000 children in Britain were admitted to care and nearly 48,000 were placed on the child protection register. A higher percentage than we ever feared have been found to abuse their own. Divorce often leads to recrimination, not only between the parents but between the children and the parent they blame most for destroying their family. Three-quarters of a million British children have no contact with their fathers as a result of the breakdown of the family home. A survey in 1996 revealed that 5–10% of young people in the UK had been homeless at some time during that year. Two of the key contributory factors were family breakdown and child sexual abuse.

It is all too easy for someone fortunate in their parents to sound glib, but the command is quite unmistakably presented as a universal moral instruction. There is no small print or escape clause. Several victims of child abuse have told me how, as Christian believers who have been forgiven by faith in Christ, they have come to a place of forgiving their parents. For as long as someone stores up bitterness in their heart, they continue to seethe with the emotional pain of past trauma. One spoke to me of a determination to 'keep my side of the relationship clean. Whatever wrong my parents have done, I will choose to show them respect.' This is very different from the emotional manipulation of some abusers, who try to use respect and shame as means of covering up their illicit activities. Those who have spoken with me are not living in denial, pretending the past never happened. Rather, they are choosing to give respect to their parents, notwithstanding their parents' wretched behaviour, because their parents, despite everything, are still due honour.

A culture of contempt

The general disregard for this commandment in our society has consequences not only within individual families, but also for the wider community. Just as the command specifically addresses the needs of our immediate forebears, by extension it applies not only to our extended family of blood relatives, but to every generation older than our own. Teachers have often observed that the way children relate to their parents determines how they will relate to other figures in authority. As the code of honouring parents breaks down in the home, anarchy breaks out in the classroom. If children have never been encouraged to show respect at home, they may scorn every effort to discipline them at school. The steady decline in respect for those in authority is demonstrated in the fact that in recent years there has been a fivefold increase in the number of expulsions from British state schools.

Some parents burst into schools, disrupting lessons, swearing at teachers and demanding that poor little Johnny be treated more fairly. Naturally their children all too eagerly honour their parents by emulating their disrespect for teachers and other authority figures. Young Johnny

notes carefully the contemptuous and hostile parental attitudes and their four-letter vocabulary, and makes every
effort to take them for his own.

Such is the increasing disregard for authority figures and
older generations that some social commentators speak of a
rapidly developing culture of contempt. The devious ways
in which politicians avoid answering questions is tedious
and frustrating, but some modern journalists are so aggressive and arrogant in turn that by the end of some interviews
it has become difficult to retain any respect for either
profession. Honouring is not the same as fawning. A journalist is not worth the name if he takes everything a politician says at face value. But it is surely possible to subject
cabinet ministers to rigorous live examination while still
showing respect for their office. The same is true of satire,
which was once understood to be the use of humour and
exaggeration with a clear moral purpose. Extreme, even
unpleasant, caricature was a means of raising issues of
principle and pursuing truth and goodness. There was an
underlying moral intent, which was to raise the standards
of public life and to honour the ideals of public service. In
recent decades, satire has all too frequently degenerated
into dragging people through the mud as an end in itself;
the underlying tone has tended to become cynical, destructive and cheap. The audience and the targets of satirical
attack are invited to wallow in the gutter together.

The West knows little about honouring the elderly. Low
pensions, inadequate housing and low prioritisation of ger-
iatric care are all hallmarks of a society that is more concerned with the cult of youthfulness than the veneration of
old age. High geographical mobility does not help. Many
caring sons, daughters and grandchildren live far away from
an aging relative who is unwilling to tear up their roots by
moving house at their time of life.

All too often the elderly have been treated as an unfortunate encumbrance, both upon the extended family and

upon the state. We all express horror when a gang of youngsters beat up and nearly kill an old lady – usually stealing about £10 from her purse. But the callous indifference and brutality of the thugs is not their problem alone – society has paved the way for their excesses of violence in a widespread disregard for the elderly. The degree to which a society can claim to be truly civilised is determined by its treatment of those in advanced old age.

In a climate of hyper-egalitarianism, some might object that honour for the young is left out of this equation. The biblical commandment is certainly not an invitation to disregard or exploit the young. Indeed Paul had to explicitly warn early Christian fathers to make every effort not to 'exasperate' their children (Eph 6:4). However, the biblical perspective does not propose an absolute reciprocity, and that is surely realistic. While a young child may at first simply learn to love, honour and obey his parents, adults have a more complex, threefold responsibility: to make it natural and appropriate for their children to honour them, by showing their children due respect; to teach their children that such honouring is a good and healthy attitude that needs to be extended to older generations and figures in authority in society; and to demonstrate a readiness to honour their own parents in ways appropriate to their age, health and present circumstances.

Models of parenthood

The conclusion Freud derived from his psychoanalytic explorations was that an individual's concept of God is nothing more than their relationship with their father writ large. To explore someone's image of God is obliquely to unveil potentially damaging aspects of their relationship with their parents. Believers therefore have much reason to be concerned by the possibility that living faith in the God of the Bible can be constrained within the distorting frame of a projected 'super-parent'.

Jesus used a distinctive word to describe the intimacy of his relationship with God. 'Abba' was the simple, childhood word for 'father' in Aramaic. It is still used by Jews today and is their equivalent to 'dada' or 'papa'. Not only did Jesus use the language of family relationships to describe his walk with God, he also claimed that this experience of God could be extended to his followers – 'my Father' would also become 'your Father' (Jn 20:17). When asked by one of his disciples to show them the Father, Jesus presented himself as the definitive revelation of the Father's character: 'Anyone who has seen me has seen the Father' (Jn 14:9). The Christian concept of God as Father therefore finds its definition not in a Freudian projection of our own male parent, but in the character of Jesus Christ as revealed in the Gospels.

Jesus' distinctive redefinition of God as Abba has a second implication that is equally profound. Since God is the first Father, the Christian understanding of human fatherhood is also to be redefined by Jesus' character. Jesus therefore becomes not only the supreme model and revelation for understanding God, but also the supreme revelation of Christian parenthood. We therefore need to learn to live as parents, not simply according to the pattern of our culture or in the manner of our own upbringing, but according to the pattern of Jesus. As the disciples related to Jesus, so we can relate to the Father by faith in his Son. As Jesus related to the disciples, so can we aspire to relate to our children. However limited our emulation of Jesus, he is our definitive example. The more we become like him, the easier it will be for our children to honour us.

Benefits for family and society

It is not difficult for us to appreciate the familial and societal benefits of building a community based on respect for parents and older generations. We can do so because we have been building a wasteland of broken relationships in the modern Western world on the opposite basis of hyper-individualism – 'Respect yourself, look out for yourself, and make sure that others get out of your way.' The consequences of this value system litter the headlines in every act of callous indifference towards the weak and the elderly.

The family, nuclear and extended, is presented in the Bible as the fundamental building-block of human society. The quality of relationships and the framework of values established within the family will shape profoundly how a child will behave in the wider community. There is therefore enlightened self-interest revealed in the promised consequences of obeying this commandment, both as individuals and for our society. In terms of individual benefits, the majority in every generation will one day be parents, and almost all of us will become elderly. As we give honour to those from other generations, particularly those older than ourselves, and as we instruct the young in the ways of honouring others, we are influencing the kind of family life and society that will have developed by the time we need to be on the receiving end, either of the care or the indifference of those younger than ourselves. This commandment is unusual in making explicit claims about the benefits that will attend those who fulfil its instruction: '. . . so that you may live long and that it may go well with you in the land' (Deut 5:16). The obverse of this commandment is all too plain: in our land it is going far from well for us at a time when our society has singularly failed to honour parents and the elderly.

6

You shall not murder.

Deuteronomy 5:17

The Sixth Commandment (i)
Unlawful Killing

The Dunblane tragedy in early 1996 cast brooding shadows over the British national psyche. On 13 March, around 9:30 am, Thomas Hamilton, armed with four semi-automatic handguns and several hundred rounds of ammunition forced his way into the local primary school and summarily executed sixteen children and their teacher before turning his weapons upon himself. The killings were ruthless, pointless and insane. As flowers and words of consolation from around the world poured into the small Scottish town, tens of thousands wept that so many innocent lives had been tragically cut short. Ron Taylor, headmaster of the school, expressed the horror of millions when he declared, 'Evil visited us yesterday and we don't know why.'

It has long been recognised that one of the most dominant cultural icons of the United States is the handgun. For many years we British looked at the dread toll of American gun slayings and declared with confident complacency, 'It could never happen here!' Today, whether in the hands of the criminally insane or the gangsters who run street crime and drug distribution, the illegal and murderous use of guns has become tragically commonplace.

In a bleak week in July 1996, further murders and

potentially deadly attacks reinforced the grim mood of foreboding throughout Britain. On Monday 8 July, less than four months after Dunblane, a machete-wielding madman rushed into St Luke's infant school in Wolverhampton, wounding youngsters three or four years old. On the same day, Jade Matthews' body was found in Merseyside. An outgoing nine-year-old, she had been battered to death on a derelict railway line just two miles from where Jamie Bulger had been killed four years previously. Jamie had been killed by two ten-year-olds. A week after Jade's murder a boy of thirteen was charged with her murder. The *Daily Mirror* captured the mood of the nation with the stark headline, 'Not Again.' Two days later, in beautiful Kent countryside, Lin Russell and her six-year-old daughter, Megan, were brutally murdered, along with their dog. They had been walking home across cornfields to the country cottage that Lin treasured as their perfect home. The only survivor was Josephine, aged nine, who had seen her family bludgeoned to death. Critically injured, she had been left in the field to die. 'Nightmare – even more horror for Britain' cried the *Daily Mail*, while the *Daily Mirror* again summed up the growing sense of dismay and even dread: 'Is Anywhere Safe?'

Meanwhile, in the East End of London, residents complained to their local council about some forty 'Jack the Ripper' tours now available to summer tourists – voyeuristic trips in which the multiple injuries suffered by the victims of this mass murderer are described in lurid detail. While the threat of murder looms ever larger, many take an evident and perverse delight in being entertained by the spectre of others' deaths, whether real or fictional.

Christian pacifism

At face value the commandment presents the ultimate Utopian ideal: no deliberate killing of another human being in any circumstances, whether by an individual or the state. Christian pacifism has always readily embraced this position, citing in addition Jesus' teaching on the need to turn the other cheek (Mt 5:39) and his express repudiation of violence even in self-defence, when Peter brandished a sword at the time of his arrest (Jn 18:11). Throughout the centuries of Christian history there has been a sustained tradition of absolute pacifism. In the early centuries, Christians certainly refused to enlist in the army of the Roman Empire. During the Reformation, Christians in the Anabaptist movement emphasised a Christian international brotherhood that came before any conformity with the military ambitions of the state. Early in the twentieth century, some Christian pacifists in London were arrested soon after the outbreak of the First World War. Their crime was distributing free copies of the Sermon on the Mount.

Unlawful killing

From the earliest days, the Jews understood the command not as a call to absolute pacifism, but rather as a prohibition of unlawful killing. Even when they were championing the Ten Commandments, the Jewish people were never a nation of absolute pacifists. They had an army and were prepared to go to war. Nor did they exclude the possibility of capital punishment. However, the laws of Moses did serve to restrict the opportunities for the aggrieved to take the law into their own hands in revenge attacks. Even that much maligned phrase, 'an eye for an eye and a tooth for a tooth', should be interpreted in this light. It is not an incitement to exact the maximum possible revenge in a spiral of escalating retaliation, but rather a means of restricting the retribution so that it remains proportionate with the original crime.

Prince of Peace

While Jesus clearly rejected violent defence of his own liberty, he was never an explicit advocate of universal or absolute non-violence for either the individual or the state. When he cleared the temple precincts of the hordes of money-grubbers, his use of the scourge did not apparently do anyone major harm, but his menacing gestures and words were clearly enough of a threat to drive the traders out before him (Jn 2:15–16). Jesus is also silent on the role of soldiers: he neither expressly commends them for their work, nor does he teach that leaving the Roman army is the prerequisite of true repentance. This ambiguity is found even at the time of the crucifixion. On the one hand it is the soldiers who torture and mock him, nail him to the cross and who gamble for his clothes with professional inhumanity (Mk 14:65; 15:16–20; Jn 19:23–24). Their cold unconcern for the wretched deaths of their victims reveals how much they have been hardened by the years of brute service as state executioners. None the less, it is also a Roman centurion, in Mark's Gospel, who provides the great punch-line of the crucifixion: 'Surely this man was the Son of God!' (Mk 15:39).

This ambiguity is also found in the early Christians' refusal to fight in the imperial army. While some historians interpret this as a simple and absolute pacifism, others suggest that the critical factor was the obligation upon soldiers to offer libations and sacrifices to the imperial gods. In that case, their principled refusal was more directly religious than pacifist, resulting not from a rejection of soldiering as such, but rather from a rejection of any kind of work that required a denial of the absolute and sole lordship of Jesus Christ.

Restraining war

The meaning of this commandment is simple for the absolute pacifist. But for those who do not accept the absolutist position, the implications of this commandment for society require careful analysis concerning what it means to prohibit unlawful killing. With regard to war, the majority Christian position over the centuries has been expressed in terms of 'just war' thinking. A war is not made legitimate by instinctive patriotism or the power of the protagonists. 'Just war' thinking transcends the crudities of 'My country, right or wrong' and 'Might is right'. To be just, both the reasons for waging a particular war and the means of warfare must meet stringent criteria.

First, *the war must be defensive*, not aggressive, seeking to protect the weak and not merely to advance the cause of the strong. Second, *the response must be proportionate*. An attack with a pea-shooter cannot legitimately be met with the retaliation of a nuclear arsenal. Third, *the warfare must be discriminate*. The target of attack must be soldiers and not the civilian population. Fourth, *the war itself must be judged to be winnable*. A suicidal prolongation of an unwinnable war is not heroic defiance but a futile waste of life. Such an approach is not restricted to external aggressors. The logic of 'just war' thinking provides an equivalent moral basis for a just uprising or revolution. 'Just war' theory, however, can never be used to legitimise murderous acts of terrorism against a civilian population.

While the absolute pacifist may be appalled at the very possibility of a just war, these principles ask searching questions of many twentieth-century wars. The First World War could not by any stretch of the imagination be called a just war, when addle-brained generals turned a generation of Europeans into cannon fodder, sending more than ten million soldiers to their deaths in the trenches. The bloodiest battle was the Somme. On 1 July 1916, 19,240 British soldiers died, with 35,493 wounded and 2,152 missing, while the German army suffered 8,000 casualties. Over 140 days the battle continued to rage between three million combatants, of whom the allies lost 794,000 and the Central Powers 539,000. The greatest amount of ground gained was seven miles, most of which was lost in subsequent battles. The world had never seen carnage so immense, so futile, so contemptible.

With the perspective of nearly eighty years, 'just war' evaluation of the First World War is inevitably censorious. Siegfried Sassoon's poem 'They', written in October 1916, is a reminder that, in the heat of battle, claims that a war is just have frequently been used to stir up loyalty in the troops and conceal the stark brutality of modern, mechanised warfare. The bishop for whom Sassoon knew only contempt was the Bishop of London.

> The Bishop tells us: 'When the boys come back
> They will not be the same; for they'll have fought
> In a just cause: they lead the last attack
> On Anti-Christ; their comrades' blood has bought
> New right to breed an honourable race,
> They have challenged Death and dared him face to face.'
>
> 'We're none of us the same!' the boys reply.
> 'For George lost both his legs; and Bill's stone blind;
> Poor Jim's shot through the lungs and like to die;
> And Bert's gone syphilitic: you'll not find
> A chap who's served that hasn't found *some* change.'
> And the Bishop said: 'The ways of God are strange!'

Turning to the Second World War, while the war against Hitler was certainly a just war if there is any meaning to the term, this does not legitimise every means of warfare. The fire bombing of German cities, endorsed not only by 'Bomber' Harris but also by Churchill, was a deliberate assault upon the civilian population, seeking to weaken the army through the collapse of civilian resolve. In Dresden, the bombs rained down a combination of high explosives and phosphorous that led to a firestorm in which 135,000 were killed. As to the bombing of Hiroshima and Nagasaki, there could be no conceivable justification for these terrible massacres under the principles of 'just war' teaching. The death toll at Hiroshima alone is estimated to have been between 80,000 and 200,000. Some try to argue that these attacks shortened the war and thus saved an incalculable number of soldiers' lives. One American airman at the time was eloquent in praise of the atom bomb: 'It was a beautiful thing. It saved many lives.' There was, however, no military need to have the first nuclear bombs fall upon cities. An uninhabited island could have served as a dread warning of what power would be unleashed without a hasty surrender. The use of these bombs therefore violated the principles of just war and broke the sixth commandment. More recently, the American use of napalm and defoliating agents in Vietnam, as well as such notorious incidents as the My Lai massacre, were further violations of the 'just war' principles, as was the sinking of the Argentinian ship, the Belgrano, with the loss of many lives, when it was manoeuvring outside the exclusion zone during the Falklands conflict.

Not all 'just war' evaluations of the policies of the victors are negative. During the Gulf War, Colin Powell had succinctly expressed the allied military objective concerning Saddam Hussein's army and in particular the crack troops of his Republican Guard: 'First we're going to cut them off, then we're going to kill them.' In the event, much to the continuing fury of some American commentators and politicians, the military advised against the complete extermination of the crushed army. Despite disagreement as to whether the allies should 'finish the job', the final consensus was that the Iraqi forces had been severely depleted and that to obliterate the Republican Guard would result in many more civilians coming under fire. Two days later the cease-fire was declared. Such restraint ran the risk of Saddam regrouping his troops, but from the perspective of 'just war' theory it showed commendable restraint. Where the taking of life is unavoidable, it should be kept to a minimum.

Nuclear pacifism

At first sight these two Christian approaches to war are altogether distinct, indeed mutually exclusive. But when we turn to nuclear weapons, the distinctions are surprisingly slender. At the height of the Cold War, the Pentagon developed a policy of absolute escalation in the event of a nuclear attack from the Soviet bloc. The inevitable consequence gave the policy its acronym: Mutually Assured Destruction, or MAD for short. Even without the ultimate folly of all-encompassing nuclear carnage, it has proved impossible to legitimise the use of nuclear weapons under 'just war' theory. Their use is unlikely to be proportionate and cannot be discriminatory. Clear thinking just warriors who are prepared to follow the logic of their own convictions find themselves obliged to conclude that they must declare themselves to have become 'nuclear pacifists'.

Church leaders have often been guilty of championing the national cause – for king and country – with little sense of a distinctively Christian perspective on the legitimacy of the particular act of war. But 'just war' theory should never be understood to be a craven endorsement of the national and military status quo. What is true for nuclear weapons is equally applicable to their alphabetic companions among the indiscriminate atrocities of the modern military arsenal: a is for atomic, b is for biological and c is for chemical. Nuclear, biological and chemical pacifism is the position of many Christian thinkers when evaluating modern weaponry against the criteria of 'just war' theory.

For just warriors to end up as pacifists in the nuclear age

has led to cries of indignation from self-styled realists. If 'just war' theory cannot cope with the brute severity of modern weaponry, they argue, the problem lies not with today's military hardware, but with the centuries-old moral theory. Perhaps we cannot afford the luxury of ethical thinking about warfare when faced with the harsh realities of the modern world. But for the Christian, the military facts of life must always be assessed in terms of the sixth commandment. This has led some to argue that it is legitimate for a nation to possess nuclear weapons, so long as they are not used. Thus, it is argued, the moral justification for the vast nuclear stockpiles of the Cold War period is found in the fact that they may well have prevented the two superpowers from ever attacking one another.

Possession without use does raise its own problems. First, no one can provide a cast-iron guarantee that weapons in the national stockpile would not actually be employed in a time of acute crisis, thereby losing the moral justification of possessing a deterrent without ever using it. Second, if a nation's enemies are fully persuaded that the nuclear arsenal arrayed against them will never be used in battle, the deterrent value of the weapons would rapidly begin to erode. Third, if deterrence is the moral justification for nuclear weapons, this does not legitimise an arms race, for all that is required is the bare minimum of warheads to serve as a deterrent.

If nuclear deterrence is morally justifiable and works in practice, then every nation state on the face of the earth can make the same case for its own nuclear arsenal. The logic of deterrence leads to the conclusion that it would be enormously beneficial, for the sake of global peace, to encourage massive, indeed comprehensive, nuclear proliferation. From the point of view of those nations already in possession of nuclear weapons, non-proliferation and test ban treaties make very good sense, restricting the dangers of weapons of mass destruction getting into the hands of terrorists, dictators and unstable regimes. From the point of view of the developing nations, such treaties represent indirect and implicit imperialism, the imposition of a global military domination by those nation states which are already members of the exclusive nuclear élite. A Christian perspective that stays focused on the essential immorality of using such weapons will call not only for non-proliferation and a test ban, but will also urge that they should continue to be phased out of the arsenals and military strategies of those nations that possess the awesome and appalling capability of mass destruction.

War crimes

The sixth commandment has further critical implications in the field of warfare. In the harsh realities of national ambitions and rivalries, wars will inevitably punctuate the history of every continent, so is the sum of Christian ethics a repudiation of some of the methods of modern warfare? Since Christians defend the principles of absolute standards of right and wrong and the reality of a final judgement, Christians also believe that the rule of law has a higher authority than the national interest. Therefore Christians are defenders not only of the need for a code of conduct in war, enshrined in our century in the Hague conventions, but also of the moral duty to prosecute war crimes.

The principle of war crimes is now well established, following the war crime trials at Nuremberg after the Second World War, even though the later trials were compromised by America's desire not to weaken the industrial and financial base of Germany once the Soviet Union had become the great enemy. US Prosecutor, Robert Jackson eloquently expressed the moral duty not to ignore war crimes: 'The wrongs which we seek to condemn and punish have been so calculated, so malignant and so devastating that civilisation cannot tolerate their being ignored because it cannot survive their being repeated.'

Regrettably, both at Nuremberg and ever since, it has almost invariably been the case that war crimes are only prosecuted against the losing side in a court presided over by the victors. We must therefore insist that unlawful killing is a charge that can in principle be laid against some of the leaders among the victors as well as among the vanquished. Those who sanctioned the fire bombing of German cities and the nuclear attacks upon Japan should have been brought to trial with the same impartial rigour as those who perpetrated the vile atrocities of the Nazis and the Japanese imperial army.

The arms trade

The final application of this commandment in the area of war concerns the military industrial complex and the huge profits to be made in the international arms trade. The British government supports the sale of arms through arms fairs and exhibitions that cost over £20 million a year. One-third of export credits go to the arms trade, even though arms represent just 1.7% of exports. When all the government contributions and subsidies are taken into account, arms exporters receive ten times as much support as non-military exporters. When Britain halted civilian aid to Nigeria in 1992, in protest against the repudiation of democratic elections, the arms trade was left intact. Developing countries now spend some £83 billion per year on arms, the vast majority of which come from the United States, Russia, China, France and Britain. Just 12% of this massive expenditure would provide clean water for all, end severe malnutrition, halve moderate malnutrition, immunise every child against the most infectious diseases and provide primary health care. In the Gulf War, British soldiers were fighting against Iraqis who had been trained by Britain until 1990, using British weaponry paid for under finance schemes provided by British banks. Iraqi soldiers even wore the same uniforms as the British, having purchased a job lot from British army surplus. There is a cynical concern with profit and power that shapes government support for the arms trade. When it comes to development aid, the same readiness to make money available is simply not apparent among most politicians.

The arms trade has a well-established line of defence for the indiscriminate sale of weapons on a vast scale. They argue the liberty of countries to defend themselves with whatever weapons they want and can afford. They emphasise the economic necessity of selling as many weapons as possible, not only to satisfy the shareholders but also to generate sufficient profits to sustain the requisite high levels of expenditure on research and development. Without open markets, they explain, no company could keep up with its competitors. Finally they point to the unrestrained approach of their competitors: 'If we decline to supply, they'll get what they want from the French, the Russians or the Americans!' The only restrictions on sales acceptable to the arms trade are the national interest and international arms embargoes (although recent cases have revealed that these restrictions are not always taken too seriously). This combination of arguments can be summed up as follows: 'In a fiercely competitive industry, ethical niceties are a luxury we cannot afford.'

The needs for restraint on the arms trade are well documented. Aid to developing countries has sometimes had strings attached that require the purchase of military hardware from the donor country. Developing nations can spend disproportionately in order to aspire to 'Western standards' of weaponry. International visits by premiers and royalty become an aggressive and seductive sales pitch for the latest high-tech weapons. The fiasco of the arms to Iraq scandal, in which British companies were given covert approval to break the arms embargo, further illustrates the readiness of governments to put profits before principle, dismissing all too readily the very limited restrictions that they choose to place on the arms trade.

Many former battlefields are now littered with thousands of land mines, resulting in years of casualties after a war has ended. The limited resources of medical care in a developing country must then be diverted to assist the resultant amputees, many of them children. The military leaders and politicians were sold these weapons as the latest in sophisticated Western technology. But now leading Western generals and military tacticians have joined in calls for this particular aspect of the arms trade to be made illegal, arguing that the sowing of massive minefields serves no significant strategic military purpose.

The trade needs rigorous policing, but the commandment takes us one step further. While it is perfectly possible for non-pacifist Christians to serve in the armed forces, assessing any particular conflict in the light of 'just war' principles, I am unable to see how any Christian can, with a clear conscience, seek gainful employment in the industry that sells the means of unlawful killing. No ethical restrictions upon use can be written into arms contracts, and so the arms trade should be a no go area for all Christians.

Guns in the home

What of the non-military use of guns? Recent decades have seen a proliferation of guns on the streets of Britain, increasingly associated not merely with major gangsters, but even with petty street crime. At the same time, across the world, single shot guns and rifles are being replaced with the latest military hardware – semi-automatic weapons that can fire off multiple rounds so fast they can literally sever limbs or even rip a body in two. More than 5,000 youths and 33,000 American adults die each year from gunshot wounds. More than a million latchkey kids come home each evening to a house where a gun is stored. The firearm homicide rate among men tripled between 1984 and 1993. Ten times as many lives have been lost as in the great polio epidemic of the first half of the twentieth century. Privately owned handguns have become a modern plague, an absurd surrender to wanton and uncontrolled violence.

The gun lobby is vociferous, nowhere more so than the United States, and their arguments are predictable. First, it is a principle of civil liberties that everyone should have the right to possess a gun. Second, shooting is a popular pastime. Lawful and responsible gun owners cannot reasonably be punished and restricted because of the excesses of criminals and the insane. Third, possessing a gun is a sensible means of self-defence when so many guns are on the streets. Fourth, legally possessed weapons are stored much more safely in the homes of responsible owners rather than stored en masse at gun clubs, where they would be more vulnerable to theft. Fifth, in the words of the British National Rifle Association, 'To say that the sport should be banned because deranged people cause disasters is to blame one million people for the acts of one madman.'

The commandment against unlawful killing leaves little credibility to such complacent arguments. The civil right to be protected from unlawful shooting is more fundamental than any claimed right to possess a weapon. Responsible users must be prepared to face restrictions in order to prevent easy access to guns for criminals and madmen. What's more, shooting and hunting do not require the rapid fire capabilities of semi-automatic pistols and rifles. As one American victim of a street shooting noted wryly: 'You don't go bear hunting with an Uzi.' The wretched statistics of the United States indicate that mass ownership of guns, legal and illegal, entirely fails to deter the use of guns. The annual death toll is a preventable tragedy, unworthy of any country that claims to be civilised. Even if it is too late for such restrictions to be introduced in the United States, in Britain it is to be hoped that highly secure gun clubs will be seen as the safest places to store legal weapons, other than those owned by farmers. It is simply irresponsible for all licensed gun owners to be entitled to keep their weapons at home.

In Australia in 1996, a madman went on a shooting rampage and the government acted with commendable swiftness to restrict as much as possible any legal access to guns by civilians. As one bereaved father said after Thomas Hamilton's massacre of the innocents, 'We cannot afford another Dunblane.' Another was equally eloquent: ' . . . for all our sakes, please, no more guns and no more worship of guns.' In a July 1996 opinion poll, 70% of British adults supported a ban on the ownership of handguns kept in the home. Unlawful killing by privately owned guns is a vice the civilised world must reduce to the absolute minimum. Farmers excepted, there is no place for guns other than single shot air guns in the private homes of a civilised society. And handguns of all kinds need to come under a total ban. To prevent a constant increase in the numbers of innocent victims, innocent sportsmen must be obliged by the law to lose their sport.

Tobacco and unlawful killing

The implications of the sixth commandment for the arms trade must inevitably be extended to other industries. Most notable is the need for tighter controls of the tobacco industry. For many years the tobacco companies denied that their product could do any material harm to smokers. The first decisive breakthrough was in 1964, when the US Surgeon General gave official recognition to the connection between smoking and lung cancer. Recent estimates by the Health Education Authority suggest that about

110,000 people a year in Britain die as a result of smoking, 30,000 from lung cancer. In the United States the estimate is about 400,000 deaths per year from tobacco-related illnesses. More recently tobacco industry representatives in the States have expressly denied any possibility that their products are addictive. Such a plea of innocence is hardly plausible, especially when some of these companies are reputed to have added extra nicotine – the addictive ingredient of tobacco – to their low tar brands in order to maximise repeat sales.

In the United States, courts have recently shown a new preparedness to order damages to be paid to smokers who have been ignorant victims of their addictive habit. Grady Carter was the first to win compensation from the industry, receiving $750,000 in damages for his lung cancer. This was the first case the industry had lost out of several hundred they have fought in the last thirty years. Just one tobacco company, BAT, made profits of $1.6 billion last year, out of which they spent $50 million on defending court cases. Thirteen separate American states are now suing the industry for the cost of treating smoking-related illnesses. The legal tide may at last be turning.

Although the adult market in the West has been in decline for several years, the teenage market continues to boom, especially among young women. The Health Education Authority survey of 1989 showed that 28% of first-time smokers are under ten and that by the age of fifteen, 24% of girls are regular smokers. The tobacco companies naturally deny that this is the result of product repositioning and the deliberate targeting of those consumer groups least susceptible to health warnings and most influenced by peer pressure. If there is no connection between marketing strategy and new growth in smoking in these sectors of the population, it is all the more extraordinary that tobacco advertising has been targeting these very groups in recent years. The total amount of press, TV and poster advertising by tobacco companies in the UK in 1990 was £87.4 million, excluding sponsorship deals (1990 Media Register).

At the same time, the industry is enjoying sustained growth in the developing world. More than fifteen billion cigarettes are smoked in the world every day, including more than one billion in the United States. From 1974 to 1987 American tobacco-related exports increased from $650 million to $3.4 billion. Tobacco export is a state-sponsored industry, supported through the Commodity Credit Corporation and the price-support system by the US Department of Agriculture. Western tobacco firms are now looking to the enormous market in the developing world, especially China, where their penetration has thus far been a minimal 10%. While the Western market continues to decline slowly, the global market is expected to grow 20% by the end of the decade. This growth would certainly be jeopardised if smoking became subject to stricter controls in the West, thereby losing any impression of being a Western, modern and stylish pastime.

In Britain, 300 cases against the tobacco companies were recently denied legal aid, and governments have been consistently weak before the power of the tobacco lobby. It seems that chancellors prefer the short-term benefits of tax revenues on tobacco products to the long-term benefits of a healthier population. Before the benefits of tighter controls on tobacco use became apparent, the tax losses would need to be made up. This would risk almost universal hostility. Any ban on tobacco would naturally provoke a massive outrage among smokers against the party in government. If there is to be real progress, it may require a cross-party initiative, when the sheer cost of tobacco-related illnesses to the country makes the present free access to tobacco intolerable.

In an unexpected development, British lawyers announced at the end of September 1996 that, despite the refusal of legal aid, they would take the cases of forty lung cancer sufferers on a 'no win, no fee' basis against Imperial Tobacco and Gallahers, who together hold 80% of the British cigarette market. The solicitors and barristers involved will have to cover both their own fees and those of other expert advisers, expected to amount to some £3 million. If they lose they would also be liable for the tobacco companies' costs – another £3 million. Their case claims that the tobacco firms failed to reduce the tar component in tobacco products once it became clear in the late fifties that tar leads to cancer for many smokers. If this case is won, many others will follow. A once impregnable industry may be on the brink of funding massive compensation, suffering a huge loss of public goodwill and severely curtailed hopes of future profitability.

In the United States, President Clinton is set to have tobacco reclassified as a drug. Such a redefinition of tobacco's status promises to have sweeping effects upon both its availability and upon the liability of the industry to compensate the victims of their product. President Clinton is said to want a ban on vending machines for cigarettes, and restrictions on advertising near schools, in magazines designed for young readers and at sporting events. He is also looking for tobacco companies to fund a $150 million anti-smoking advertising campaign. Only by Western legislation can there be effective protection of those consumers most susceptible to the continuing allure of tobacco: the young and those in developing countries.

Such restrictions are long overdue, but in the meantime we must note the cynical and callous addiction to profits that has caused tobacco companies to redirect their marketing. When middle-aged Westerners know too much about the health risks for the market to grow, they simply redouble their marketing to those groups to whom the risks are least well publicised, who are therefore least well suited to resisting tobacco's addictive but ultimately deadly allure. The tobacco industry is based upon a knowing violation of the sixth commandment. To continue to derive enormous profits from a drug that is known to result in premature death for many of its users is nothing less than unlawful killing.

Death by video

The media increasingly indulge in an unrestrained orgy of unlawful killing by proxy. In an age of spectacular, computer assisted special effects, the camera can linger long upon the simulated deaths of the silver screen. The slow motion and pause buttons on every video recorder reinforce the opportunities to dwell upon gory close-ups that once would have sickened and horrified. Our imaginations are invited by TV, video and cinema to feast upon unlawful killing by proxy. Dustin Hoffman and Roger Moore are among the leading actors who in 1996 have expressed great concern that Hollywood has finally gone too far, declaring that they are sickened by the degrading excesses of recent movies. Although the violence is glamorised, the agonising pain of the victims is hardly ever conveyed. Nor is attention given to the overwhelming sadness of the bereaved. Almost every one of those 38,000 American deaths by gunshot wounds results in many other deeply traumatised lives. But in Hollywood the guns normally just go 'bang' and it's all over.

What was once designed to shock has now become the staple diet in adult movies. What was once unacceptable has now become normal. And does this matter? Of course it does. Those who feast on unlawful killing in the imagination become desensitised to the brute realities of life, slipping more easily into excessive, depersonalised and callous treatment of others. In one recent grisly case, a fourteen-year-old British boy used a nine-inch bread knife to try to cut off the head of a woman he had previously tied up with telephone cable. At his trial he explained that he was obsessed with the movie *The Predator* in which an alien strips its human victims of their flesh. High on LSD, he was acting out the violence of his favourite movie. All distinction between reality and fantasy had been blurred. His girlfriend was equally indifferent to their victim's fate, egging him on with the cry, 'Hurry up and get it over with.' After she stabbed the victim five times, they left her for dead and ran off with £300. Remarkably, Margaret Dennison escaped with her life and was later able to give witness against them in court, albeit in a hoarse whisper.

The issue is no longer one of artistic freedom and creativity. Men and women are making big bucks out of the make believe of unlawful killings: up close and in your face. In 1992, *TV Guide*, a magazine listing television schedules, estimated that there are an average of ten acts of violence during every hour of broadcasting. The American Psychological Association has estimated that 'the average American child who watches 3 hours of television a day, has by the age of 13 witnessed 8,000 murders and more than 100,000 other acts of violence. By the age of 18 those numbers have jumped to 40,000 murders and 200,000 other acts of violence' (*The Independent*, 25 October 1993). Voices of decency and sanity have got to begin to cry out that this is not artistic freedom; it is a degrading excess, in which life is cheap and the innocence of children is being stolen from them.

Similar criticism must be laid against the more sensational TV programmes that recreate violent crimes. In the UK, TV watchdog authorities have begun to criticise such programmes which reproduce violence not so much to catch the criminal as to titillate the jaded palates of the viewers, for whom a real-life murder recreated on screen provides another variant in the diet of unlawful killings in the imagination. Murders on celluloid are the late-twentieth-century equivalent of the fights to the death in a Roman amphitheatre: more hygienic, but just as remorselessly barbaric and just as destructive to the dignity of the human spirit. In watching, we are all degraded. The tide of violence needs to be turned back on our screens. And in video stores, those violent movies that are not banned – and many more deserve to be – should be made available from restricted outlets or higher shelves. All too often at present, young children searching for the latest family film in many large video stores are obliged to run the gauntlet at child's eye level of the massed ranks of lurid video boxes advertising the excesses of violence or soft porn. The command against unlawful killing warns that we urgently need to clean up our act.

Computerised killing

What is true of cinema and television is also true of computer games. As the technology becomes photo-realistic, many of the most popular games involve shooting or physically assaulting human beings, frequently with the deaths celebrated in sensational and vivid detail. Such games perpetuate several myths. First, death is never final: when you lose, you die, but there's no pain and at the press of the restart button you begin again. Second, the death of others is an achievement to be enjoyed, regretting nothing. The deaths are not only the necessary means of achieving the objective of the game, mere obstacles to be swept aside, but killing is to be applauded, an achievement that is to be celebrated, bringing the rewards of special screens, triumphal music and additional points towards a high score.

When the game play is centred on killing other people, the line is blurred between imagination and reality. The games reward a callous indifference to the fate of others, a swift reaction that kills and takes no prisoners. There is no place for conscience, concern or remorse that others have lost their lives. Computer simulations of battlefields may prove the ideal training ground for tomorrow's soldiers, training them in hair trigger responses and sharpening their will to obey orders and fulfil their objectives. Any real-life combatants may eventually seem no more significant than those they have previously eradicated on a virtual reality screen. Once again there is a need both for legislation and for personal vigilance. What kind of society is it that encourages young children to enter the killing fields in their bedrooms every evening and then be rewarded for their carnage with a place on a high score table?

Parental protection

So far in this chapter we have identified possibilities for national policy and legislation. But there is also a vital place for parental vigilance. Children will always want to pretend they are playing with guns. If nothing plastic comes to hand they may use their finger, a suitable twig or some building bricks. To attempt to prevent all such play would be naïve. Kids will be kids. But a line can be drawn between innocent fantasy and replica guns. In our own home, while water pistols have always been a source of much fun, we have never allowed realistic replica guns to become part of the arsenal of children's toys. We do not want to blur the line between children's fun and the brute realities of unlawful killing. In the same way, computer games where the combatants are alien creatures and the destruction is not dwelt upon in lingering and loving detail have been deemed acceptable, but not those games where the enemy requiring urgent eradication is a fellow human being. The commandment about unlawful killing speaks not only to the military, but also to violent excesses of the imagination that often find easy access to almost every Western home.

Capital punishment

In previous generations, the legitimacy of capital punishment as a useful means of upholding the rule of law was taken for granted in the West, by Christians and non-Christians alike. Four classic reasons have been recognised for the imposition of custodial sentences on convicted criminals. Society is *protected* by removing the criminal's freedom. There is an opportunity for the criminal to be *reformed*. Others are *deterred* from committing similar crimes. Fourth, the criminal is *punished* for the wrongs committed. The impact of post-war liberalism has tended to create a fashionable consensus that repudiates the notion of punishment as a decidedly secondary or even unacceptable reason for imprisonment. None the less, the great majority of ordinary people still instinctively look for a 'punishment to fit the crime', so that the mass-market newspapers are filled with moral outrage when a judge is unusually lenient in the sentence imposed for heinous criminal acts. At the same time, the established consensus among politicians in Britain, but not everywhere in the United States, is that capital punishment is essentially barbaric, entirely unacceptable as an expression of the rule of law in a modern liberal democracy. For the Jews, there was no difficulty in exacting capital punishment despite the commandment about unlawful killing. While individuals were not entitled to seek revenge personally, the Mosaic law unequivocally gave the state the right to take life.

The emotive arguments for and against capital punishment make for a lively debate. On the one hand we are asked, 'Would you not want the execution of a murderer who had killed in cold blood your closest family members?' On the other hand the question is posed, 'Would you seriously be prepared to execute someone yourself in the name of the state?' Such subjective approaches provide more heat than light and are incapable of providing a coherent, rational basis for national judicial policy.

The evidence remains decidedly less than conclusive when we consider the crime patterns of countries that do or do not employ capital punishment. Those in favour of restoring the death penalty can point to the enormous escalation in the number of murders in Britain since the abolition of hanging. However, many other factors have contributed to the rise in violent crime in the last forty years, so the specific impact of the absence of the death penalty is all but impossible to quantify. Abolitionists on the other hand point to the United States as proof positive that the death penalty simply does not work as an effective deterrent, since its availability in at least some of the states is accompanied by appallingly high, indeed by European standards almost apocalyptic, levels of violent crime. Once again the data are inconclusive: we just don't know whether a society like the United States, given the vast numbers of guns in private hands, would suffer from even more murders without the 'ultimate deterrent' of the possibility of state execution.

The Bible has no hesitation in speaking about right and wrong, crime and punishment. Since Jesus taught plainly that there would be punishment beyond death, the Christian need make no apology for stating that punishment is a legitimate dimension of a criminal's sentence, alongside protection, reform and deterrence. So what of capital punishment? In principle, the ultimate sanction can fulfil three of these criteria, even though it can hardly be said to make a useful contribution to a criminal's reform! To be sure, a convict awaiting execution may choose to repent and to prepare for the final judgement, but the concept of reform is usually taken to signify a change of lifestyle that will be worked out this side of the grave.

The great and irrefutable criticism of the death penalty is that no court is infallible. The successful appeals on behalf of convicted murderers not only in Britain but around the world have revealed the possibility of errors in the judicial system, and still worse possibilities of deliberate corruption and miscarriages of justice. Particularly when faced with highly emotive crimes, such as acts of terrorism and the murders of children and police officers, the police and the courts can evidently be placed under extreme pressure to secure rapid convictions. In Britain the release of the Birmingham Six and the Guildford Four, many years after their original convictions for mainland IRA bombings, are stark warnings that even a judicial system that prides itself on its rigorous fairness can fall into disastrous error. At the time of the prosecutions, the public mood would readily have cheered a decision to send these supposed terrorists to the gallows. As a result, any successful appeal would have led to the grossly inadequate result of post-humously cleared names for those wrongfully executed. Some leading politicians have suggested that the occasional miscarriage of justice is a risk that we have to take for the sake of upholding the rule of law and minimising the number of murders in our society. But any abuse or mis-taken imposition of the death penalty is surely nothing more than yet another unlawful killing.

Faced with these dilemmas, many have come to the conclusion that while in principle the death penalty is the ultimate sanction of the state in enforcing the rule of law, in practice the risks of a mistaken conviction, however small, mean that the actual use of the death penalty should be avoided. Some have argued that the death penalty be restricted only to terrorists or to those who kill police officers, but the evidence of successful appeals in recent years demonstrates that such convictions may be at parti-cular risk of being unsafe. The death rows of some parts of the United States are a wretched disfigurement of a civi-lised society, in which convicted murderers string out their days from one appeal to another, with the threat of execu-tion constantly held over them and never either exacted or withdrawn. This surely is a crueller fate than the death penalty itself, leaving the criminal in a half life, stripped not only of liberty, but of dignity and hope. There may however be one class of murderer who could reasonably and appropriately be subject to the death penalty, and that is the mass murderer who is found guilty beyond all reasonable doubt of a whole series of unlawful killings. Many are unable to see any good reason to keep such a person alive and incarcerated for several decades.

The Sixth Commandment (ii)
The Beginning and the End of Life

So great is the significance of the sixth commandment for our society, that we could not possibly address all the most pressing implications in a single chapter. The issues of abortion and euthanasia will therefore be explored in this separate chapter drawn from the sixth commandment.

Abortion

It is a curious irony of the last thirty years that the liberal consensus that has worked strenuously to oppose the right of the state to take the lives of convicted murderers has also unstintingly defended the greatest taking of life since the Jewish holocaust. In 1967 Britain accepted new abortion legislation that thirty years later has resulted in 600 abortions every single day. In the United States, there are no fewer than 4,000 abortions each day. The ostensible concern in the British legislation was with exceptional cases: where the mother and baby's lives were already at risk; in cases of severe deformity; where the pregnancy had resulted from rape or sexual abuse; where the continued pregnancy would cause grave psychological harm to the mother. The great emphasis at the time was upon the need to do away with the dangerous hazards of illegal back street abortions, particularly to protect the poor.

The sheer volume of abortions in the West today indicates that abortion is now being widely used as an acceptable means of contraception. One in four British women aged between sixteen and twenty-four has had an abortion. Between 1968 and 1991 over 3,500,000 abortions were carried out in Britain. One in five children conceived in the United Kingdom is aborted – in the States it is one in four. *Newsweek* has estimated that there are currently 1,500,000 abortions in the United States each year (*Newsweek*, 7 October 1996). As many American babies are exterminated every four years as the total population of Greater London, Wales or Denmark.

The latest government statistics in 1996 revealed that the highest incidence of abortions in Britain is found among the wealthier suburbs of the South East. It is now not among the urban poor but among the middle classes that abortion is most likely to occur, which suggests that social convenience and an uninterrupted career have become determinative factors in opting for abortion. Back street abortions have given way to back door abortions, in which the intended restricted access of the 1967 legislation has been effectively ignored or reinterpreted by the medical profession in response to the demands of patients. In Britain there are now 184,000 abortions per year, of which 98% are performed for 'social' reasons. The intention of the abortion legislation was to legitimise the procedure in specific and exceptional circumstances. Today, in many parts of Britain, pressure from those with unwanted pregnancies and the compliance of many doctors has resulted in abortion on demand.

A further disturbing trend was revealed in October 1996 by researchers at City University, New York (*The Times*, 12 October 1996). For many years abortion has been presented as much safer than live birth, but new statistics suggest that abortion increases the chances of breast cancer by one third. The reason seems to be an excessive exposure to oestrogen that does not occur with a natural miscarriage. Joel Brind, Professor of Endocrinology at City University has estimated that abortion now results in no fewer than 5,000 cases of breast cancer in the United States every year. It takes time for breast cancer to develop: the years that have seen a massive increase in the numbers of legal abortions are still too recent for us to have been faced with the resultant and parallel increase in breast cancer. By the middle of the next century the annual rate of breast cancer arising as a result of an abortion is set to rise to 25,000 each year. An unexpected and potentially deadly price tag has been discovered for women who have abortions.

The headline-stealing case in Britain in the summer of 1996 concerned a mother who was expecting twins and asked for one of them to be aborted. The story was leaked to the press, indicating that the abortion had not yet taken place and that the mother was unmarried and in 'straitened circumstances'. She needed the abortion, it was explained, because she could neither cope with nor afford two additional babies. If she could not have a selective abortion, she would ask for both to be aborted.

Uproar resulted in the media, with several individuals and charities offering money to assist with the upbringing of the child and some couples offering to adopt the unwanted twin. The hospital then explained that they were unable to pass this information on to the mother, since this would compromise their obligations of confidentiality. As a result, one charity sought an injunction to prevent the termination until the mother had been told of these compassionate offers. The hospital was then obliged to disclose that the abortion had already been carried out several weeks before. More details were then made public, with the explanation that the doctor had lied in order to protect his patient's confidentiality. The woman was not after all a single parent but happily married. What's more, she was not living in poverty, but was middle class, married to a company director.

Several alarming factors arose from this case, despite the assurances of the British Medical Association that it raised no new ethical issues. First, the hospital was revealed to have concocted a web of lies. While the intention was to protect confidentiality, it brought into question the integrity and trustworthiness of the medical profession faced with a controversial procedure. If the doctors involved could not be relied upon to tell the truth, could they really be entrusted to make complex ethical decisions concerning their patients' legal and medical status? Second, the hospital had originally sought to hide the controversy behind the suggestion that the decisive factors were the income level and marital status of the prospective mother. This begged the question as to whether financial status could ever be a legitimate basis for an abortion. If so, beneath what income threshold would this eligibility for an abortion come into force? Third, grave questions were left unanswered about the possible trauma for the surviving twin, who may one day need to come to terms with the discovery that they were the fortunate survivor in a random selection of a victim in the womb. This could lead to acute feelings of rejection by the mother and of guilt for surviving at the expense of their fellow twin.

The most serious consequences concern the very principle of a selective termination, when there was no other threat to the life of either twin or their mother. The decisive factor in the abortion was the fact that the second baby would apparently have been 'inconvenient' for the family. If it is acceptable to abort one twin on such a pretext, others may in due course explain that to have a child of the 'wrong' sex would be so traumatic for the mother that a termination is the only 'kindly' remedy. Indeed selective terminations already appear to have become customary in some parts of the Indian sub-continent, with such frequency that the male–female ratio of new births has become significantly distorted. In due course, the possibility of even more sophisticated pre-natal tests may allow parental choice to be exercised with regard to intelligence levels, or such trivia as right- or left-handedness or the colour of hair or eyes. As one MP noted, this was a major step in the direction of creating 'designer babies'. Abortion on trivial grounds threatens to turn babies into the ultimate life accessory, whose survival beyond the womb will be determined by the personal preferences of their mother. 'Doctor, I cannot possibly keep this baby. I've already booked an exotic holiday for next summer, and the photos would be ruined if I was eight months pregnant!'

When a charity sought an injunction to defer this particular abortion, it was roundly criticised by many commentators on two counts. First, it was accused of interfering in the private life and personal moral decision of this particular mother. There is of course a right of private judgement. If someone wants, for example, to receive cosmetic surgery, there is no reasonable right for others to interfere with that choice, even though some may wonder whether such use of money is altogether wise and advantageous. Behind this complaint of unjustifiable interference are the assumptions that all moral values are personal and private and there is no such thing as a universal moral framework. In post-modern culture, it is assumed that we need to work out our own relativistic moral guidelines, while never imposing our personal preferences on anyone else. Where relativism is deified, the only remaining sins are intolerance and interfering with someone else's private moral code.

The second argument has been dominant in abortion debates for a generation, namely that it is a woman's inalienable right to choose. Abortion has been politicised as an expression of feminism. To be feminist is to seek liberation from the constraints imposed upon women by men. Since an unwanted or unplanned child would impose severe limits upon the freedom of any woman, many champions of this new freedom argue that women must be freed from the chains of the legal and moral constraints that have been imposed by male-dominated societies. To be against any abortion, the more extreme feminists argue, is to be against all women.

The essential question is whether choosing an abortion is as much a private decision as choosing to have a face lift or a pedicure. The duty of the state is to defend the vulnerable. In order to protect the safety of the weak, restrictions are imposed upon the liberty of the strong. A car driver must sacrifice the right to enjoy the top speed of his car in a built-up area, in order to protect the lives of pedestrians. A gang of football fans must give up their enjoyment of alcohol at matches, in order to protect the safety of those who would be at risk of the consequences of drunken violence, above all innocent bystanders, in particular children and the elderly. If we accept that the baby in the womb has its own rights as a human being, then the rights, choices and preferences of the mother must be held in balance with the rights of the unborn. Since the baby is the more vulnerable, in no position to defend itself, the state has a duty of care to protect the unborn. This duty to protect the vulnerable is not an indefensible intrusion into private choice that deserves to provoke widespread condemnation. Rather, it is a hallmark of a civilised society that restrictions are set upon the liberty of the strong in order to defend the rights of the weak. Women's rights must certainly be asserted and defended, as equal citizens in the eyes of the state and as equally made in the image of God. But babies in the womb, female and male alike, have rights too. It is a woman's right to choose whether to get pregnant. Once a new life has been conceived, its future existence is no longer a private matter for the mother but a public concern for a humane and civilised society.

Further revelations in 1996 concerned some controversial methods of late abortion and the nature of life in the womb. The medical profession has preferred to shield the general public from the grisly details of abortion techniques. Late abortions in particular require a very physical, indeed aggressive, extinction of life. In the 'partial birth' method, the infant is partly born and then the skull is pierced and a tube inserted through which the brains are sucked out until the head collapses and life is extinguished. C. Everett Koop, the former US Surgeon General, has stated that this type of abortion is never truly medically necessary. In a previous draft of this chapter I reiterated on trust the claim frequently repeated in the British press that this exceptionally cruel and ruthless means of executing a baby was reserved in the States only for a very small number of late abortions where severe disabilities had escaped early detection or where the mother's life was in imminent danger. Unfortunately this turns out to be a reassuring cover-up. One clinic in New Jersey is rumoured to perform up to 1,500 of these abortions each year, although a spokesperson has denied this total. *Newsweek* estimated that several thousand partial birth abortions occur every year in the States (*Newsweek*, 7 October 1996). The *Washington Post* surveyed American doctors in late summer 1996 and discovered that this procedure is most frequently used in abortions performed upon young, poor, single women with no health problems, who simply want an abortion in the second trimester.

A second technique was made public by the BBC in spring 1996, and was said to be frequently used in the States but only employed in Britain in a limited number of private hospitals. Once again it is a technique for late abortions, but this time the procedure takes place within the womb. Small forceps are introduced, not to assist with delivery but to seize hold of an arm or a leg. The baby is then quite literally torn limb from limb, each fragment dropped into a disposal bag until the collection of body parts is complete. The procedure has been summed up by a stark phrase: 'dismember and evacuate'. Not a single drop of anaesthetic is provided to numb the child before dismemberment. There is a vileness to such brutal executions in which the carcass of a baby is disposed of with indifference equal to that of a cosmetic surgeon disposing of unwanted globules of body fat.

One senior doctor defended the use of dismemberment as a means of abortion. First, he said, there is no proof that the foetus in the womb is capable of experiencing pain, and so he preferred to work on the assumption that no pain is felt unless clear proof is found to the contrary. Second, he explained that in a traumatic accident, such as a severe car crash, the nervous system goes into a state of shock, as a result of which the experience of the full enormity of the pain is delayed. Such patients frequently do not appreciate the full extent of their injuries until several hours after the trauma itself. Therefore, he explained, we can be reassured that the baby who is being torn limb from limb will almost immediately enter a profound state of shock so that the infant will have died long before the possibility of experiencing the full extent of the pain has arrived.

Many will not only be shocked by such a technique of abortion, but also sickened by a medical practitioner offering such specious and callous arguments. Those who have been trained as guardians of health and life have become routine executioners in the abortion clinics. If a murderer was facing capital punishment, and the prison governor explained that he would be torn limb from limb, there would be a public outcry, even from many who argue passionately for the restoration of the death penalty. If the prison doctor justified the method on the grounds that the condemned man would not feel very much, because his nervous system would almost immediately be numbed by traumatic shock, the public would hardly be reassured. Rather, the doctor's resignation would be demanded, with a widespread sense of public disgust that, for the sake of personal gain, he had prostituted his medical credentials and completely lost sight of the essential dignity of every human individual. A civilised society would not tolerate the execution of the most notorious murderers by the callous techniques of modern abortion. If such methods of killing were used on farm animals, enraged protests would break out around the country.

These methods of abortion are not the standard procedures, although the brain evacuation or 'partial birth' method is attractive to some as a cost-cutting exercise, since it requires only one day's use of a hospital bed. Up to nine weeks, a mother can take three tablets to induce a miscarriage. Many think this method is the least distressing for both mother and child. However, many expectant mothers are unable to decide upon an abortion within the first nine weeks. A second method brings on premature birth by use of the drug Prostaglandin, and may be used up to twenty-four weeks. By this time a foetus is viable outside the womb, and the Royal College of Obstetricians and Gynaecologists has recently warned doctors about the legal implications. If a child is born alive as a result of this treatment and then dies, the doctors may be subject to a murder charge. A third technique accounts for some 85% of abortions in Britain, and may be used up to thirteen weeks. This is the suction method, in which the infant is vacuumed from the womb. The suction apparatus tears apart the baby, whose body parts need to be counted and reassembled in the operating theatre in order to assure that the evacuation is complete.

Not only are we discovering more about the methods of abortion, we also know far more than a generation ago about life in the womb. New techniques of photography allow us to see the development of a baby, and we know that after just a few weeks the new life is instantly recognisable as a human being, with delicate little eyes, hands and feet. Pictures of a tiny baby sucking its thumb in the womb demonstrate visibly that what we are considering is not an impersonal blob, but a child in miniature. Just as the military have developed an impersonal language to cover up the consequences of weapons of mass destruction, so that civilian casualties are spoken of as 'collateral damage', the medical profession prefers to speak of foetuses, not babies; of termination, not killing. But the victims are babies and the consequence is death.

As well as being able to photograph life in the womb, medical science is also able to keep premature babies alive at an ever earlier stage of development. As a result, the latest week of pregnancy in which abortion can be undertaken legally has been made earlier. When TV news programmes show pictures of a twenty-four-week-old baby fighting for life in an incubator, assisted by all the expertise and devoted care of the medical profession, there is a revolt of the imagination against the thought that, on another floor of the same hospital, babies at the same stage of development, just as unmistakably a human child, have been aborted on a regular basis in Britain for the past thirty years.

The most significant revelation in 1996 concerned not the methods of late abortion, but the development of the nervous system in the womb. Ten years ago most doctors believed that newborn babies were unable to feel pain. In May 1995 a report on foetal pain commissioned by the Health Department concluded that before twenty-six weeks a foetus was unable to feel pain because its brain and neurological system were not yet sufficiently developed. New evidence from medical research was presented to MPs in July 1996, by medical scientists in Britain, Ireland and Australia. This new report demonstrates that babies in the womb not only react to external stimuli, but they do so in ways that have established the fact that, long before birth, a baby is capable of experiencing pain.

Professor Fisk, of Queen Charlotte's Maternity Hospital, has measured levels of cortisol, a stress hormone, when blood samples are taken from a baby in the womb. He has discovered that the hormone level rose sharply when the needle was inserted. Others have filmed a foetus apparently recoiling from a needle in the womb. More than that, it appears that in the womb as well as after birth, a baby may actually experience pain more acutely than adults, since the hormonal reactions are more intense. The methods used to kill babies in the womb certainly cause them as much pain as they would an adult. It now begins to look as if it may well hurt them even more than such savage ways of extermination would hurt an adult victim.

The convenience of abortion and the doctrines of hard line feminism will not necessarily prevail against such stark realities. Paul Johnson, writing in the *Daily Mail*, drew a parallel with a previous social ill that had stripped vast numbers of people of their human rights. As society woke up to the evils of slavery, society may yet wake up to the unleashed horror of mass abortion (*Daily Mail*, Friday 16 August 1996). Slavery had previously seemed beyond rebuke to many Westerners, being advantageous in wealth creation and even beneficial to the enslaved. Eventually, the socially advantageous became the morally indefensible, with the recognition that the law could no longer tolerate the possibility of treating a fellow human being in ways that stripped him of essential dignity and liberty. Just as society repudiated the tyranny of slavery, it is to be hoped that society will also repudiate the holocaust of the womb. Unborn babies are human beings too.

The command against unlawful killing demands tighter restrictions upon the availability of abortion. But are there ever circumstances in which abortion is justified? Is the right to life absolute, or are there circumstances in which a life can legitimately be sacrificed? Should both the mother's and the child's lives be at risk if the pregnancy is continued, abortion is undoubtedly a legitimate option for the mother. Of course, even here there are exceptions. One British woman hit the headlines when she was offered chemotherapy to combat her cancer, but the therapy would kill the baby she was carrying. The hospital proposed an abortion followed by cancer treatment, but the mother chose a different course of action. Since no treatment could absolutely guarantee her own health, but her baby was not at risk until an abortion was suggested, the mother decided that she should first carry the baby to term and then begin her own treatment. Such courage and self-sacrifice, placing a higher value on her baby's life than her own, is a remarkable, indeed heroic, exception in our increasingly self-centred age.

The other least contentious circumstances, where abortion may be deemed the lesser evil, are when the pregnant woman is no more than a child, when the pregnancy is the result of rape or sexual abuse, and when the baby is suffering from severe and life-threatening disability. In the cases of rape and abuse, no one could reasonably impose upon the mother a legal duty to carry the baby to term. However, since the baby is not only the result but also a second victim of the sexual assault, should the expectant mother be prepared to preserve the child's life she deserves universal commendation and support.

In the case of disability, the tendency has been to make abortion normative not only for immediately life-threatening conditions, but also where there is a prospect of such conditions as Down's syndrome or spina bifida. The increase in pre-natal diagnosis of genetic disorders means that the number of reasons to abort will multiply rapidly in the next few years. In many cases the diagnosis will be statistical – a certain degree of likelihood that a disorder will occur. Many parents have already been alarmed by the medical pressure to agree to an abortion in such circumstances as the normal and more or less automatic solution. Doctors can only provide one treatment for most genetic disorders diagnosed in the womb, and that is abortion.

No one can doubt that responsibility for a disabled child is enormously exacting for parents. In some cases, adoption or care away from home is a necessary provision when parents simply cannot cope. However, at a time when abortion has become the all but automatic consequence where any degree or kind of disability is diagnosed, we have to ask some critical questions. Do disabled people have a full and reasonable claim to human rights? At what levels of disability is abortion an expression not of compassion, as it is often presented these days, but rather an act of discrimination and prejudice? For many doctors, abortion has been the automatic solution where Down's syndrome has been diagnosed. Some are now questioning this knee-jerk reaction, given the evident quality of life enjoyed by many with this disability. They are often among the friendliest and happiest of people.

Alyn can never leave his wheelchair and cannot eat, drink or go to bed without the assistance of his full-time helper. Until his mid-teens he never spoke, and it was assumed that his mind was as crippled as his body. Now he has studied successfully at two universities, he is a published poet and has spoken to audiences of several thousand. If Alyn's physical condition was diagnosed in the womb today, his mother would be strongly recommended an abortion as the only reasonable and humane course of action. Some would suggest that to carry the baby to term would be very selfish, giving life to a child without true human dignity and bringing an unfair financial burden upon the state. But no one can credibly suggest that Alyn does not have as much right to life as any other human being. Even though his lucid and creative mind is trapped within an unruly body, he shows greater mental sharpness and agility than many of his able-bodied friends.

Abortion is an intensely emotive issue. The headlong rush of our society to normalise abortion for the slenderest of reasons can produce a backlash of utter indignation. In defence of the rights of the unborn, some protesters in the States have taken to picketing abortion clinics, pressurising pregnant women not to go through with their abortion and attacking abortion clinic staff. The three most notorious protests in recent years all occurred in the States in 1995. A surgeon who carried out abortions was shot and killed in Massachusetts, and one month later two women attending an abortion clinic in Virginia were shot dead. Such actions need to be repudiated unreservedly, for they have no place in the reasoned defence of the biblical commandment against unlawful killing. It is quite absurd to take a life unlawfully in the defence of those unlawfully killed. Women on the brink of an abortion, however much their decision may be regretted by others, have every right to be protected from verbal and emotional assault.

There are initiatives to be taken in defence of the unborn, but they always need to be law-abiding, constructive and respectful of others. Counselling services can be provided for those women faced with an unwanted pregnancy who want to explore alternatives to abortion. People prepared to adopt unwanted children need to be identified. Support rather than rejection needs to be offered to women who have chosen to have abortions, for many still struggle years later with intense and secret feelings of shame, guilt and regret. Above all, politicians need to be lobbied and a new public debate needs to be encouraged, making the case that the pendulum has swung too far so that abortion has become too casual and too common a procedure. When Britain is killing 600 children in the womb every day, there is blood on our hands and shame on our hearts. The most dangerous place to be alive today in the Western world is not the car-congested streets of a major city or even under the missiles of a war zone; it is within a mother's womb. The place of intimate nurture and protection has become the place of greatest risk to life.

The value of life

In the very first chapters of the Old Testament the irreducible value of every single human life is affirmed. We are not valued more or less highly in the eyes of God according to our gender, our race or our generation. Neither physical prowess nor beauty, neither intelligence nor achievements, neither social status nor income qualify us to be of higher value than another. Every single human being is made in the image of God. Therefore, as long as a human being is alive, each one of us deserves the same treatment, with respect, dignity and the right to a life protected from the threat of unlawful killing. This principle applies equally to the elderly, those with disabilities and babies in the womb.

In the case of babies in the womb, the question therefore arises, 'At what point are these human rights conferred?' One traditional answer was that fullness of human life is achieved at birth. However, modern medical science permits us to examine life in the womb and to monitor a child who is already living. What's more, we now have some measure of control in determining when labour begins. To suggest that human rights are conceived at birth seems quite arbitrary. No one today would seriously suggest that any time up to the onset of labour the foetus lacks any claim to protection under the law.

If we trace the life of the foetus before labour begins, some draw the line at viability. Thus, in Britain today, once a baby is viable outside the womb, it may no longer be subject to abortion as freely as in the earlier months of pregnancy. Medical advances have meant viability is now possible at an earlier stage of development, as a result of which the last week of pregnancy in which an abortion is permitted in Britain has been reduced from twenty-eight to twenty-four weeks. While such modifications of the law are to be applauded, there is an underlying problem if the conferral of human rights is made dependent on the provision of modern medical support. On the basis of viability outside the womb, a baby in London or Los Angeles qualifies for human rights several weeks earlier than a baby in Lagos or Guatemala.

Many use the phrase 'a potential life' to describe the status of the foetus before viability is attained. However, if we ask when the specific chromosomal make-up of a particular individual is determined, the answer can only be at the moment of conception. From that moment, individual particularity and uniqueness are already determined. 'Potential life' is therefore a term more accurately reserved for sperm and unfertilised egg cells. They have no more than the potential to fuse and produce the complete genetic code of a distinct human being. That is why most non-Catholic Christians have no hesitation in commending contraception. Indeed, I would go further and say that, with the population explosion still threatening to overwhelm many parts of the developing world, and with AIDS still exacting its deadly toll, any attempts to prevent the universal availability of contraception in the developing world are nothing less than perilous and ill-informed. However, that is not for one moment to justify the scandalous human rights abuses of the Chinese regime, where compulsory contraception, abortion and even sterilisation have all been part of their totalitarian policy of population control.

There is a common objection to the claim that human rights begin at conception. Many will observe that, since by no means all fertilised eggs are implanted in the womb successfully, and since many pregnancies miscarry, it is surely legitimate for medical science to bring about deliberate failed pregnancies – 'We are only mirroring nature.' This is an altogether specious argument. Before the days of inoculation and modern hygiene, the infant mortality rate was very high, but this does not legitimise us killing children under five. Many women used to die in childbirth, but that does not mean that the labour ward is a legitimate place to despatch unwanted women. Many men used to die in their forties, but that cannot legitimise mid-life euthanasia. There is no logic to this argument. Death by natural causes at any stage of life cannot legitimise death by human intervention. From a biblical perspective, the command against unlawful killing applies from conception to the last day of life, because human rights are not conferred upon us because of what we can do or whether we can fend for ourselves. Rather, human rights are conferred because of who we are – men and women made in the image of God, even from the moment of conception. The sanctity of life, from conception to death, must be emphatically affirmed and defended in an age of casual slayings, not only on the cinema screens but in the abortion clinics of the Western world.

Frozen embryos

In July 1996 a new kind of killing commenced in Britain – the eradication of frozen embryos – provoking *The Independent* to the memorable headline: 'A world of anguish in an inch of glass.' Some 3,300 embryos were due for destruction on government orders, issued by the Human Fertilization and Embryological Authority (HFEA). Each embryo comprises four to eight cells, and is no bigger than a full stop. They have been frozen since 1983, as *in vitro* fertilisation usually produces far more embryos than can be returned safely at any one time to the patient's womb.

New legislation has decreed that these frozen embryos, known by some in the medical profession as 'frosty babies', should be destroyed after five years in storage, unless the people who provided the original sperm and egg cells contact the clinics and give their consent for extended storage. The embryos are defrosted, and then a drop of water or alcohol is added which makes the cells disintegrate. The process is completed by incineration, under protocols for 'the disposal of human biological material'. The embryos are being destroyed as the waste products of infertility treatment.

Nine thousand embryos had been created before August 1991, for which 900 cell donors had refused to reply to letters or had proved untraceable. Of those who responded, 8% asked for their embryos to be destroyed, 15% donated them to other couples, 30% kept them for their own future use, and the rest agreed to make them available for medical research. While the headlines were concerned with the 3,300 due for destruction, this meant those set aside for medical research were equally denied any right to life. One mother who had children by IVF and donated her eggs to other parents reckoned that leaving them to research was worse than destruction – 'I wouldn't want my children experimented on.'

Reactions were vigorous. The Vatican denounced the policy as a 'pre-natal massacre'. David Alton MP declared, 'If this is life, as I believe it is, then surely we should be giving the childless the chance to adopt in the womb.' Lord Winston, director of the *in vitro* fertilisation clinic at Hammersmith Hospital, West London, was emphatic in defence of the policy: 'You can't give away someone else's genetic material without their approval and express permission.' Ruth Deech, chair of HFEA, was equally robust: 'Some have suggested that these embryos should be donated or adopted. This would be wrong, both legally and ethically.'

The policy was incongruous. In abortion, a father's consent is not required for the abortion to occur, nor can his wish for an abortion override a mother's wish to keep the child. But this disposal of frozen embryos required the active consent of the father as well as the mother for life to be preserved. Many problems were documented in the press. Some received their consent forms too late, through administrative error. One couple living overseas faxed through their request for prolonged storage, but it arrived twenty-four hours too late, and the destruction had already taken place. Hospitals were unable to trace some patients, particularly those who had moved overseas. One couple had been transferred to the United States with the Air Force, but the clinic could not ask the Air Force for their new address because that would have compromised patient confidentiality. Similarly, a patient in Britain had changed her doctor, but the hospital could not ask her new doctor for an up-to-date address. In these cases, no contact was made, and the embryos were destroyed without consultation. An estranged husband declined to sign the forms because he wanted to avoid any future liability to pay maintenance and wanted to start a family with his new partner. His estranged wife was distraught, fearing that this might be her last chance to have a child, but she was helpless. One man's wife had died and he wanted their embryos donated to other couples, but he was told this was probably not possible, since his wife was 'unavailable' to give her consent. Finally, there was the problem of anonymous donors, many of whom either could not be contacted or had no wish to be drawn into further responsibility concerning sperm or eggs they had long since donated. This catalogue of incongruities reveals that the present law is botched: it is incompetent and lacks credibility.

The ethical issue that lies behind this mismanagement can be bluntly stated. If the frozen embryo is a piece of property, it belongs to the provider of the egg and sperm. It therefore represents no more than a couple's potential to have children and has no intrinsic rights of its own. On this basis, it would be wrong to offer for adoption a potential life that belongs wholly to its natural parents. However, if the embryo is a potential person, it ultimately belongs to no one. If the embryo already has the right to life, then the chief responsibility of the state is to protect the life. The embryo should then be unlocked from its frozen state as soon as it is not wanted any more by the original patients, not for destruction or research, but to enter fully into life, made available for adoption. From one perspective, the issue can be reduced to spare part disposal, of no great moral significance. From the other, we have unleashed nothing less than a pre-natal massacre, driven not by ethical considerations about the sanctity of life, but by advances in medical technology that have produced frozen embryos that are surplus to requirements. This is not a problem that will go away. Nine thousand frozen embryos reached the five-year limit this summer. But there are another 51,000 frozen embryos in Britain alone. If the same ratio persists, another 18,700 embryos are already destined for destruction, with perhaps half the rest set aside for use in medical research. If such figures provoke a continuing sense of outrage in the country, the law will simply have to be changed. It is an extraordinary reversal of customary procedures to say that a life will be terminated unless the mother and father make an explicit request for the embryo to be preserved. This slaughter of the innocents represents another step away from the Judaeo-Christian commitment to the sanctity of every human life.

Euthanasia

When life is so greatly at risk in its beginnings, many of the arguments about removing life can also be applied to the elderly and the terminally ill. Particularly when the baby boomers retire and a small working population are faced with supporting an ever larger and longer lived number of the elderly, the argument is very likely to be advanced that, beyond a certain number of years and a certain degree of enfeeblement, the elderly will have come to place an intolerable burden upon their families and the state. Just as some now argue that human rights are conferred incrementally upon the unborn and are only fully secured at birth, others are likely to begin to argue for the gradual removal of human rights in the 'economically unproductive' years of extreme old age. Any legislation that permits voluntary euthanasia is likely to move imperceptibly towards normative and therefore more or less compulsory euthanasia, as the elderly feel ever more keenly a sense of guilt at still being alive, with a consequent need to 'volunteer' for termination.

The terminally ill raise distinct problems. The medical profession has a duty of care towards the sick, but this should not be confused with a duty to prolong life under any circumstances. The blunt reality is that some who are kept alive without hope of recovery today would long since have died less than a generation ago. In the case of those who are only kept alive by a life support machine, a distinction must be made between switching off a machine and active euthanasia. When a patient has no hope of recovery it is, in effect, a mere semblance of life that is sustained by artificial means. Active euthanasia, on the other hand, proposes a direct medical intervention to bring about death. When the machine is switched off, a patient is allowed to die. Whenever a deadly cocktail of drugs is administered, the patient is unlawfully killed.

Patients suffering from PVS – persistent vegetative state – raise further dilemmas. These patients are understood to have lapsed into a waking coma as a result of massive brain damage, from which there is no reasonable prospect of recovery. Some continue to live without the assistance of a life support system, but their continued existence is dependent on others feeding them. In the case of so-called 'vegetables' who are totally dependent on a life support system, turning off the machine represents the removal of medical assistance that is no longer able to provide any hope of recovery. In the case of those in PVS, the prolongation of the residual fragments of their life may seem equally futile, pointless for the patient, emotionally draining for their family, and expensive for the state. In England, it was the case of Tony Bland, a victim of the tragedy at Hillsborough football ground in 1989, whose case brought about a change in the law after a ruling in the House of Lords in 1992. For the first time, the hospital was given legal clearance to remove the hydration and feeding apparatus. The comatose patient was left to dehydrate and starve to death. Since then, at least seven others have been allowed to die through similar, deliberate neglect.

A debate continues as to whether this was a humane death or whether it marked the crossing of a boundary preparing for the full legalisation of euthanasia. For the family there was no doubt: great relief was expressed that the young man had been allowed at last to complete his death. Nonetheless, two concerns remain. First, there is a distinction between the removal of medical care that is no longer useful and the removal of feeding. We need to ask whether this active promotion of death is really within the duties of the medical profession. Second, while modern medical equipment has sometimes had the result of prolonging the mere remnants of life, where death has been deferred there is always the possibility of an unexpected recovery. In 1996, at least three cases were reported in Britain where patients diagnosed as being in a persistent vegetative state, that is beyond all prospect of recovery, have enjoyed a sudden and inexplicable awakening. In one celebrated case, a man came out of his coma and promptly described the assailant whose attack had brought on the condition in the first place. Eddie Kidd, the British motorbike stunt rider, also amazed doctors in September 1996 when he emerged from a coma seven weeks after a jump that went disastrously wrong. His wife had been told that he might stay in a coma for several years, but he surprised everyone when he opened his eyes and was able to recognise family members.

Such recoveries, however rare, point to the need for great caution in diagnosing a condition beyond hope of recovery. Hospital representatives gave the immediate reassurance that these cases had obviously not been diagnosed properly; a genuine PVS is indeed irreversible. This explanation would not be at all helpful faced with the need to decide whether your own close relative should be starved to death, because it always leaves open the possibility of another misdiagnosis and recovery. Even if such removal of feeding is legitimate, and that remains a matter of controversy, we need to have an absolute confidence in the reliable and definitive diagnosis of a persistent vegetative state before such deadly intervention should ever be contemplated.

The most recent evidence from the Royal Hospital for Neurodisability in Putney, Southwest London, is still more disturbing. According to their report, published in July 1996, 40% of patients considered to be in a persistent vegetative state were aware of their surroundings but unable to communicate. Of those who were misdiagnosed, 65% were blind, and so unable to respond to such standard tests as blinking in response to a threat or following an object with their eyes. Most were severely paralysed and could only respond with small bodily movements that could easily be missed when they were lying down. Therapists have found that many could remember their past lives and communicate through a simple electronic buzzer. This means that people have been treated as insentient vegetables when they are fully aware of what others are saying and how they are being treated. One of the mistaken diagnoses had been confirmed by three of the most eminent experts in the country. As a result of this study, new guidelines are needed to ensure that misdiagnosis does not lead to wrongful killing.

In an editorial in the *British Medical Journal*, Dr Ronald Cranford, a neurologist from Minneapolis, defended euthanasia for those wrongly diagnosed as being in a persistent vegetative state: 'I would speculate that most people would find this condition far more horrifying than the vegetative state itself, and some might think it an even stronger reason for stopping treatment than complete unconsciousness.' This demonstrates just how assertive the movement for active euthanasia has become. The argument in cases of PVS was that the patient was effectively dead already. Now the pro-euthanasia lobby are extending the argument not only to include extreme pain, but also a perceived severe reduction in the quality of life as a reason for non-consensual euthanasia. One of the Putney report authors, Dr Keith Andrews, responded that 'quality of life is something I have, not something you tell me I have'. His plea is direct and clear: 'You have to give people the opportunity to live before giving them the opportunity to die.'

One of the most astonishing coma cases of recent years was Sarah Mapes, a pregnant woman, whose coma was the result of a blood clot on the brain. At the request of her parents, Sarah was kept alive on a life support system in order to give her baby the chance of life. She died four days after the Caesarean delivery, but her twenty-eight-week-old baby survived. Sarah's partner, Steven Davies, was furious. He wanted Sarah to die without delay and take the baby with her, but his preferences had no legal status since he and Sarah were not married, so the wishes of Sarah's parents prevailed. Steven is now caring for the baby but is expected to sue the hospital for keeping the baby alive. In his view, Sarah was 'not treated as a person, she was just a human incubator'. The priority of the grandparents was the preservation of life where that was possible, deferring the inevitable death of their daughter for the sake of the child in her womb – 'We thought that if we couldn't keep our daughter alive we must do everything possible for our grandchild.' The hospital is to be commended for keeping Sarah alive for the sake of the baby. To have ignored the baby's right to life would have been a grave dereliction of duty. They were treating not just one patient but two, and the greater concern had to be for the one with the opportunity to survive.

Australian Bob Dent made the headlines in September 1996 when he took his own life with the aid of a computer. When he pressed 'yes' in response to the final question from the computer, he had thirty seconds to wait before a deadly cocktail of drugs was injected into his bloodstream. Within a minute he was dead, the first legal suicide under the Northern Territories Euthanasia Law. Many other patients from across Australia and overseas are reputed to be planning to move to the Northern Territory in order to commit legal suicide. It is set to become the euthanasia capital of the world.

This controversial legislation requires that a patient must be over eighteen and suffering from an illness that is incurable and fatal. Doctors have to fulfil twenty-two requirements before approving euthanasia. A psychiatrist must confirm that the patient is not suffering from a treatable clinical depression. The illness must be causing severe pain, and the doctor must have explained the available treatments, including palliative care. The patient must be of sound mind, making a voluntary decision, having considered the implications for the family. Time is also provided for second thoughts: a seven-day delay from the formal request until the certificate is signed by the patient; a further forty-eight hours before the equipment that will kill the patient is set up; then come the three final chances, when the computer asks the fatal question: 'Do you wish to proceed?'

No one can dispute that Dent was in great pain, nor that

Dr Philip Nitschke who assisted in the suicide was acting in what he took to be the best interests of the sixty-six-year-old who had terminal cancer. For Dent, the new euthanasia law was 'the most compassionate piece of legislation in the world'. The pro-euthanasia perspective is also championed by the Liberal premier of Victoria, Jeff Kennett, who declared, 'For people to be able to die with grace and dignity at their choosing, as opposed to suffering, is just beautiful. Life is about choice. Death should be about choice. And politicians ought to butt out.' Other Australians are implacably opposed to the new legislation. Prime Minister John Howard is supporting an attempt in the national parliament to overturn the territory's law. The Roman Catholic Archbishop, Edward Clancy, declared that he was 'deeply ashamed that Australia should be the only country in the world to legalise the killing of an innocent person'.

In Britain, voluntary euthanasia is due to be debated again in parliament within the next year. The British Medical Association remains opposed to euthanasia, but a survey of 750 doctors in September 1996 revealed that 46% wanted the law to change and one-third would be prepared to help a terminally ill patient to die, if it were lawful. In Australia, it is claimed that many doctors outside the Northern Territory are deliberately flouting the existing law, practising euthanasia unofficially. There is no statistical data to reveal whether this illegality is also occurring in Britain or other countries. What is clear is that the tide of popular and medical opinion is turning, and that euthanasia seems likely to become legal and indeed normal within a few years across the face of the earth. In the week of the first legal suicide in Australia, the studio audience for BBC Television's *Question Time* were asked whether they thought voluntary euthanasia should be made legal: 35% said no, 47% said yes, with 18% undecided. Where abortion has undermined the sanctity of life, euthanasia is an inevitable consequence, unless the argument can be won against the tide by those who are convinced that, despite the intention to be compassionate, it is nothing less than another form of unlawful killing.

The dignity of life, in sickness and in health, points towards a distinct priority in the care of the terminally ill: neither the merely mechanical postponement of death nor death's acceleration through direct intervention, but the preparation for death with dignity through the provision of palliative care. The hospice movement has paved the way in developing more sophisticated approaches to the management of pain among the terminally ill.

Palliative care has not always been favoured in mainline hospitals, where the priority is naturally active intervention to cure the patient, and 'mere painkilling' can seem like a final admission of defeat. There is also much fear in the medical profession of the addictive tendencies of powerful painkilling drugs. We should seek to provide every medical support for those who are dying, remembering that the dying are unlikely to be particularly concerned about the dangers of long-term addiction to painkilling drugs. But we should not begin to play God by assuming the right to decide when anyone should be made to die. Palliative care is genuinely patient-centred care for the terminally ill in a way that euthanasia can never be.

Whether we are considering weapons of mass destruction, the tobacco industry, representations of death in mass entertainment, abortion or euthanasia, the commandment against unlawful killing stands out against many of the modern norms of behaviour in our death-crazed society. When modern technology can do so much both to enhance and to destroy, protection and respect for life need to be championed as never before. The sixth commandment has lost none of its force if we hope to build a truly humane and civilised society in the twenty-first century.

7

You shall not
commit adultery.

Deuteronomy 5:18

The Seventh Commandment
The Price of Free Sex

The development of national obsessions can be analysed by measuring how often they appear in the newspapers. The two rising stars of the first half of 1996 were the lottery, up 22.3% on the first half of 1995 to a total of 5,499 articles, and divorce, up 43.5% to a total of 3,940. If this trend continues, love of money will sustain the national obsession with the lottery, but divorce looks set to become the UK's primary obsession by the summer of 1998 (*The Independent*, 16 July 1996). Britain has become the divorce capital of Europe. One in three marriages ends in divorce, 10% of marriages break apart within two years, and 25% of divorces involve those who have remarried after a previous divorce.

Five factors have been identified that make divorce statistically more likely, although none makes the failure of a marriage inevitable: if the couple are teenagers; if the bride is pregnant; if one of the couple has previously been divorced; if one of the couple has divorced parents; and, finally, if they have been living together before marriage. This last factor is particularly striking, contradicting what has become the present-day convention and received wisdom in Britain. For a generation our society has conducted a social experiment in which living together has often been justified as a sensible preparation and precaution – a kind of trial marriage in order to test out compatibility without the complications and finality of a legally binding marriage contract. One of the characteristics of living together is that the relationship is provisional, and it now appears that this attitude tends to be carried over when a couple who have been living together decide to get married. The unforeseen and hazardous result of living together is that the subsequent marriage can actually become more tentative and disposable.

Biblical sexuality

To suggest that the reason for the seventh commandment is that the Bible is anti-sex is absurd. The sexual dimension of marriage is affirmed in Genesis 2 and emphasised in the New Testament by the apostle Paul and above all by Jesus. The Song of Songs is a glorious erotic masterpiece, celebrating the gift of sexuality. To be sure, the church suffered a monumental distortion in its understanding of sexuality under the influence of platonism. This led to the absurdities of the medieval church, in which the married state was considered intrinsically inferior and less spiritual than the condition of celibacy. In the twentieth century, the Protestant free churches have tended towards the opposite extreme, getting perilously close at times to implying that the married state is intrinsically superior to singleness, and practically excluding single people from active participation or full-time ministry.

A parallel can be drawn with contemporary secular culture, which has often implied, or even blatantly asserted, in magazines, films and popular music, that the only way to enjoy a fulfilled life is, while not necessarily to be single or married, certainly to be sexually active. A sexually promiscuous life has become the touchstone of illusory fulfilment – but those who are sexually active have never actually experienced automatic, instantaneous and total fulfilment.

However, in our society they certainly feel entitled to look down upon those who choose to refrain, above all those who have decided to preserve their virginity. This myth of fulfilment through sex is sustained and reinforced through the fantasies of Hollywood adultery, which is almost invariably spontaneous, successful and athletic. Beautiful 'body doubles', the sexual equivalent of stunt men and women, reinforce the fantasy: everyone is doing it, and it is easy, good for you, harmless fun and gymnastically fulfilling.

The biblical approach sets high value on human sexuality, but emphatically speaks about 'love-making' rather than 'having sex'. The sexual dimension of marriage is specifically affirmed in the Bible as something that is more than physical encounter. It is an expression and a strengthening of love. There is a depth to sexual intimacy that is ultimately more important than whether the 'earth moves' during every encounter. In complete contrast to the fervent intensity of the modern pursuit of technique and multiple orgasm, love-making is more about belonging than achievement. The more a couple belong together in intimacy, the more profound their experience of sexual union.

According to the biblical understanding, when a couple are married they become 'one flesh'. What this signifies is a permanent covenant of commitment and love. When someone marries, their essential identity is expressed in the marriage; the man is not intended to dominate or subsume the woman, but they enter a commitment in which they retain their individuality and yet they experience a new union. Marriage is not a secondary aspect of life, no more significant than a liking for golf or mushy peas, but it is intended to become intrinsic to a new sense of self.

Charles and Diana's amatory and adulterous escapades illustrate a very different attitude to marriage from the biblical approach. Charles' defence of his confessed adultery was that it was predicated upon the failure of his marriage; that is, the adultery didn't cause the marital breakdown, but followed after it and was justified by it. As another participant in a celebrity affair commented to the *Daily Mail*, 'She [the adulterer's wife] knows he is having a sexual relationship with me . . . I am separated, so I am effectively a single woman. So far as I am concerned it is all above board' (*Daily Mail*, 22 July 1996). This modern understanding of the self as essentially distinct from the marriage was precisely defined by Eileen McGann, whose husband, Dick Morris, a White House political adviser, resigned over assignations with a prostitute. McGann, a highly regarded trial lawyer, decided to stand by her man, but in an interview with *Newsweek* she clearly expressed the fact that her sense of self was distinct from rather than intrinsic to their marriage: 'I have my own life, and I shared part of that with Dick' (*Newsweek*, 30 September 1996).

Alan Storkey, author of *Marriage and Its Modern Crisis*, has summed up this modern understanding of marriage that is far removed from the biblical concept of commitment: 'Marriage is seen as external to the individual and their attitudes and feelings, so if anything goes wrong, people give up on this external relationship and keep their inner quest going' (*New Christian Herald*, 24 August 1996). From the biblical perspective, the specific circumstances of a marriage are immaterial. If someone who is married has sexual relations with a third party, that activity is wrong and its name is adultery.

Within a biblical understanding, human sexuality is a positive gift from God that is wonderfully enriching, but it carries the potential for enormous harm if indulged casually, beyond the rightful confines of marriage. Because we are integrated beings, there is no such thing as sex without consequences. Sexual union causes us to bond deeply with the person with whom we make love.

Therefore any sexual union outside the marriage relationship is a dangerous thing. There is no such thing as a casual fling. The adulterer bonds with their lover, and the marriage partner feels a deep sense of betrayal. The contrast could not be clearer. To the modern world, adultery is provisionally wrong, a temporarily inadvisable option that will become available once again should the marriage relationship begin to deteriorate. From within the biblical concept of a binding commitment and an intrinsic shift of identity into the 'one flesh' of marital union, the seventh commandment allows no exceptions. Adultery is always and intrinsically forbidden and wrong.

The consequences of adultery

The authenticity of the biblical perspective is seen in the devastation that adultery causes. Anyone who has had to deal with adultery in the family, or provide support for a friend, will recognise the familiar pattern. Adultery hurts so much because it is a fundamental betrayal of trust in the foundational human relationship between a husband and wife. That is why the British political convention is wise when it requires an exposed adulterer to resign from the government. If a man or a woman cannot keep their promises to their spouse, there is every reason to doubt their suitability for public office, because their essential integrity has been found wanting.

The betrayed partner usually moves through a predictable cycle of traumatic reactions. Shock and numbness will give way to a sense of betrayal. Feelings of betrayal may then be followed by self-blame, as they wonder what they must have done to somehow provoke or fail their partner. Anger will in time turn outwards upon the betrayer and their accomplice in adultery, sometimes erupting in uncontrollable and even violent rage. Fantasies of extravagant revenge may then sustain the injured party through a profound sense of inner vulnerability. Finally a resolution will be found. For some years, the instinctive resolution has been to file for a divorce, the sooner the better. Some American counsellors detect the possible emergence of a new trend: choosing to stay together for the sake of the children or because the process of divorce and a readjustment to singleness has proved infinitely more painful than many once imagined, when there was less widespread experience of the emotional price of separation and divorce.

The betrayed are entitled to seek divorce – Moses and Jesus both endorsed that option. But divorce inevitably brings its own emotional cycle of betrayal, self-blame and anger; any children will go through a similar cycle of emotional trauma, since it is impossible to protect them entirely from the traumas of marriage breakdown; and all of this maelstrom of betrayal and loss, regret and even revenge will be garnished with the protracted hostilities of legal confrontation. No one should pretend that marital faithfulness is always easy. If it were, the commandment would be irrelevant. But nor should anyone pretend that adultery does not have unpredictably painful consequences or that divorce can ever be a painless termination to a failed marriage. In expressing and controlling our sexual appetites we have the capacity to enter the heaven of marital union or the hell of adultery and lust.

Licence and containment

There is no escaping images of sexuality today, both illicit and condoned, but as standards continue to slide there is a rising tide of complaints. Advertising hoardings in Britain were the setting for the 1996 'bra wars', in which rival manufacturers combined photographs of scantily clad and sultry-eyed young women with suggestive copy lines. Following a barrage of complaints, the Advertising Standards

Authority required the most provocative wording to be withdrawn.

The Broadcasting Standards Council recently criticised TV soaps for their preoccupation with teenage sex. The Council expressed particular concern about programmes transmitted in the early evening, when very young children would be watching. A complaint was upheld against an episode in *Neighbours* in which a teenage couple openly discussed their sexual relationship and the young man made explicit reference to using a condom. A motel bedroom scene with a pair of lovers in *Heartbreak High* was also censured. Such programmes can easily convey the implication to an impressionable young audience that to become sexually active is a mark of maturity, and therefore something to pursue as early as possible. Although the programme makers might argue that they are simply reflecting the trends of modern living, the danger is that such programmes set the trend, redefining what is acceptable, desirable and normative through the stories they choose to portray.

Reg Varney, veteran star of TV comedies, summed up growing public disquiet at the declining standards on British television: 'I do not like heavy swearing and dramas where the bird's got all her kit off at the drop of a hat. I'm old fashioned. I'm a family man. Some of the stuff on television now is near enough pornographic' (*Daily Mail*, 24 July 1996). With the digital revolution imminent and satellite and cable systems already in place, Europe is on the brink of an enormous increase in the number of available TV stations. It seems inevitable that a number of these will be tawdry, others explicitly pornographic. Governments may be powerless to stem the tide, with satellite broadcasts threatening to cross national borders without restraint, beyond restriction by national legislation or international standards of decency. In the movies, films like *Showgirls* and *Striptease* continue to blur the line between Hollywood and soft porn. The old adage is that sex always sells, but as mainstream films have become more explicit, many have been surprised that such films have not met with greater box office success.

Even unemployment offices, now euphemistically known as Jobcentres, have become embroiled in the trend of becoming inappropriately explicit. *Jobsearch* is a magazine available in sixty Jobcentres around the country. The mid-July issue gave space to job opportunities not previously mentioned in its pages: in between adverts for cleaners and clerical workers, the unemployed were promised a substantial income working from home as prostitutes. Ian McCartney, the Opposition employment spokesman issued a public complaint: ' . . . this magazine invites vulnerable men and women who are unemployed to take up prostitution as a business opportunity . . . instead of proper employment and training opportunities.' The chief executive of the Employment Service, Mike Fogden, made an extraordinary defence of the magazine, suggesting that the liberty of the unemployed would somehow be infringed if pimps could not advertise for recruits. Fogden said that if anyone was offended they should complain to the Advertising Standards Authority: 'It is not for the Employment Service to censor publications or deny job-seekers access to the widest range of job opportunities.' On this tattered logic, we might expect Jobcentres to begin to carry adverts for mercenaries or bit parts in porno films. Sanity prevailed, and a government minister overruled the chief executive, ordering the immediate withdrawal of the magazine.

Westminster City Council faces one of the highest levels in the country of illegal advertising for prostitutes. Nearly seven million cards publicising prostitutes are placed in Westminster's public telephone kiosks each year. Street cleaners have seen the number of cards they remove increase from 50,000 to 150,000 per week during the last five years. They are often replaced in minutes by 'carders' who claim to earn more than £100 per day for their work. As the cards become increasingly explicit, British Telecom has been receiving a rising number of complaints from phone users who find the brazen and explicit cards an offensive intrusion upon public decency. In summer 1996, BT announced a new policy to eradicate the cards. The numbers on the cards will be phoned, with a warning that the adverts must be removed. Any recurrence and the phone number will be blocked so that no incoming calls can be received.

While BT seeks to get prostitutes' adverts out of its phone kiosks, Chief Constable Keith Hallowell is a senior police officer concerned to get the prostitutes off the streets. His approach is revolutionary in Britain, for he has called for the legalisation of prostitution. The arguments in favour of legalisation are clear: prostitution is inevitable, so it needs to be contained and controlled by the state; official red light districts would protect innocent householders from the double disgust of having street-walkers outside their door and being approached by kerb-crawlers; state-run brothels would provide protection for the prostitutes from abusive customers and cruel pimps; they would also ensure regular health checks, keeping sexually transmitted diseases at bay. Some might add that the police have an impossible job at present: if the prostitutes are moved on, they will simply set up in another street; when they are arrested, they go back on the game to pay their fine. The police have neither the money nor the available personnel to achieve a massive crackdown on prostitution.

The arguments against legalisation are equally forceful: a 'black market' of illegal prostitution would be likely to continue alongside state-run brothels, so the health risks and problems for innocent householders would continue; if the police are not able to get prostitutes off the streets now, there is no reason to suppose they would be successful after legalisation; by legitimising selling sex for money, legalisation would encourage more women to become prostitutes and more men to use them and so the emotional and relational health of the nation would be worsened acutely; unless the state brothels were located in the middle of an industrial estate, in which case few would use them, they would result in massive, distasteful and permanent disruption for ordinary householders, wherever these state brothels were established; children's charities have identified a frequent link between child sexual abuse and subsequent entry into prostitution – legalising prostitution could result in more casualties drifting into a lifestyle that reinforces their experience and self-image as sexual victims.

The seventh commandment reminds us that the ultimate argument against legalisation is not pragmatic but moral: prostitution and the use of prostitutes are morally wrong. We therefore need to insist that both the sellers and the purchasers of sexual services need to be faced equally with the full force of the law – the men who seek out prostitutes have too often been treated lightly. This sordid trade will never be eradicated, but it should be kept to the very margins of society. Two government initiatives would be welcome. First, a consistent and sustained policy of public disgrace for successfully prosecuted kerb-crawlers and other users of prostitutes, featuring their names and photographs in a 'page of shame' in local newspapers. Second, a rescue programme for convicted prostitutes, who would be given the choice of paying a fine as at present or attending a state-sponsored residential centre for rehabilitation, where they would have an opportunity to come off any drugs, prepare for a new kind of employment, and consider moving to another part of the country to escape the destructive influence of their former associates. The legalisation of prostitution would represent a disastrous loss of moral conviction in the nation. You don't solve a problem by surrender.

Excesses demanding control

Just one generation ago many theatre-goers were shocked by the nudity in the stage productions of *Hair* and *Oh! Calcutta!*. By the summer of 1996, the latest £1 million raunchy musical in London's West End was described as offering very little plot and a great deal of nudity. The performers included a lesbian female quartet from the States, who were previously banned from performing in London by Westminster Council, due to their explicit simulated sex acts. However, under a bizarre distinction in British law, a council can prevent a 'performance' but has no control over a 'play', so the quartet returned to London to perform thanks to this legal loophole. The director, Michael Lewis, described the show as 'full nudity and stage sex done in the most tasteful way'. He added, rather unnecessarily, 'It does not have a great political message.' The show's impresario, Michael White, said that he would like audiences to leave the theatre 'wanting to have sex, with whatever and whomever' (quoted in *The Times*, 23 July 1996). The producers of *Voyeurz!* expressly rejected any comparisons with the seedy sex shows of Soho, but the descriptions of their production leave little doubt that the comparison is accurate. Their show is sordid in content and depraved in intention. It represents one more lurch into the gutter for British musical theatre.

One of the most disturbing developments of unrestrained access to pornography in recent years has been the World Wide Web. The Internet is not at fault in itself – it is simply a means of conveying information, as morally neutral as a printing press, a blank piece of video tape, or a telephone. Almost instantaneous access to information from across the world is a new phenomenon, and governments have not yet established effective means of controlling the distribution of undesirable data. The two most notorious categories are child pornography and information useful to terrorists. Paedophiles are said to have mobilised to provide information and despicable photographs via the Internet. The web site widely denounced for aiding and abetting international terrorism provided detailed instructions on how to make various kinds of home-made bomb.

In the summer of 1996, Singapore led the way in censoring the Internet. The list of sites their national agency has banned is posted on the computers of all the Internet service providers in the country, with the result that no one in Singapore can access these sites. Civil liberty groups have expressed the concern that this censorship could be extended by totalitarian governments to ban not just pornography, but any other kind of information they consider undesirable, leading to a repression of free speech. Extreme libertarians consider all forms of censorship to be intrinsically wrong and a denial of individual human rights. Most people will undoubtedly accept that a modest restriction of personal freedom is a small price to pay to exclude pornography, especially child pornography, and incitements to terrorism. There is a moral crusade to be fought for the protection of children, and governments need to be urged to adopt methods of control for the Internet, via the national service providers, as soon as possible.

Teenagers and sex

As teenagers in the West continue to enter puberty earlier, the period of adolescent pre-occupation with sex is prolonged. We have already noted the pressures implicit for the audience when characters in teenage TV soaps are engaged in sexual experimentation. Earlier we referred to the increase in child prostitution in Britain, with girls as young as eleven working the streets. Some youth clubs today are not only freely dispensing leaflets about 'improving your drug abuse', but are also dispensing contraceptive advice and free condoms. Of course children need to be protected from accidental pregnancies and the danger of AIDS and other sexually transmitted diseases, but little care or concern is being invested in protecting them from premature sexual activity. Sexual maturity is emotional as well as physical, and those who do too much too soon can carry the emotional scars for years. For young women there is an additional risk: the incidence of cervical cancer is significantly higher among those who become sexually active at an early age, even more so for those who have many sexual partners.

The recent film *Kids* is a classic example of ambiguity in the movies, with its scenes of under-age, drug-induced and abusive sex. Is it a serious work of art, asking provocative questions? Or is it exploitative, both of its young cast and of the young audience that it seeks to attract? Does it, in Hamlet's phrase, set a mirror up to life? Or does it glamorise and commend extreme forms of sexual licentiousness? For some critics it was a masterpiece, for others soft porn. Politicians generally kept their heads down and avoided the controversy.

Pop music has always tended to recommend self-indulgence as the only acceptable virtue for the young, but recent years have seen more and more songs making explicit and unambiguous references to having sex. One of the most popular albums of 1996 included one track about getting high on drugs and another about oral sex. In recent years, mid-teen magazines have come under increasing scrutiny, faced with similar charges of inducing premature sexual awareness and promoting a casual, achievement-oriented attitude to sexual activity. Sensational stories of unusual couplings, explicit guidance on techniques and orgasms, invitations to experiment – these have become the standard bill of fare for a generation of teenage girls. Their parents have failed to provide a coherent moral framework that commends sexual restraint, and so the children are all too easily convinced by the media that their virginity is a problem in need of urgent cure. Parents face an immense responsibility in this collapse of sexual morality. Who will protect our children from the enormous potential destructiveness of unrestrained sexual appetite and activity?

The *Daily Mail* gave voice to a sense of alarm in the nation over this growing crisis in sexual morality, with an unusually long front-page headline in July 1996: 'Pregnant at 15, married at 16, and divorcing at 17. Just what does this girl's story tell us about morality in Britain today?' (*Daily Mail*, 22 July 1996). The next day *The Times* ran an unrelated story shot through with the same concern and anxiety. In a searching critique of the fashion industry, Jane Gordon warned that young girls aged ten to fourteen are probably more vulnerable to commercial exploitation than any other age group. They think of themselves as seventeen and dress accordingly. Clothes shops market the latest fashions in cut down sizes: crop tops and hipster shorts, Lycra miniskirts and flimsy slip dresses. Jane Gordon even discovered in some shops child size copies of sexy silk underwear. The line between girlhood and womanhood has been deliberately blurred by the fashion industry, so that young girls are pressured to become unknowing nymphets, accidental Lolitas, conforming with a style of dressing that gives them 'a sexual allure they do not understand and cannot handle' (*The Times*, 23 July 1996). The deliberate commercialisation and exploitation of children and young teens is stripping childhood of its pre-sexual innocence and pressuring children to think of themselves in sexual terms and to become sexually active at an ever earlier age.

The UK charity Childline has revealed the hidden pain of modern childhood. In the last ten years, its helpline has received half a million calls. In September 1996 it estimated that it was receiving 10,000 calls per day, although only 3,000 got through because the demand had become so acute. While some of the calls concern loneliness and broken hearts, drug abuse and bullying, the majority are a cry for help from victims of abuse, both sexual and physical.

In the United States, Douglas Varie, a zealous thirty-two-year-old prosecutor in Idaho, has uncovered a 1921 statute that he is attempting to use to turn the tide of promiscuity. The state law decrees: 'Any unmarried person who shall have sex with an unmarried person of the opposite sex shall be found guilty of fornication.' This is an uncontentious definition of the unmarried equivalent to the sin of adultery. What is more unusual is the fact that the fornicators in Idaho can now be fined up to $300 and jailed for six months. Varie is concentrating on using the law against teenage offenders. One of the first, Amanda Smisek, age seventeen, pleaded not guilty at her trial, but the fact that she was seven-and-a-half months pregnant counted against her and she was found guilty. Amanda was only fined $10 (£6.50) by the court, which was clearly understanding of her misdemeanour, but she was also put on probation for three years, which presumably means that she is one of the first American teenagers for many years to experience a legally enforced period of sexual restraint, at least until her twentieth birthday. Whatever the good intentions in Idaho, it is impossible to imagine such legislation being enacted, let alone enforced, elsewhere. If a credible alternative to sexual licence is to be found, it will need to be commended by other means.

Child prostitution is one dimension of the crisis in sexual morality where government initiatives are welcome and required. More than a million children worldwide work in this deplorable trade, which has become a multi-billion dollar industry. The brothels of India and Thailand hold countless children as prisoners, many in cages. Some are kidnapped, some taken as bond-slaves to pay off a family debt. Others are brought to prostitution by desperate poverty, with their parents or an older sibling acting as their pimp. The impact of AIDS, from which many of these wretched children are now dying, has increased the demand for younger prostitutes, who are presumed to be healthier, but children's skin breaks more easily than adults', and so the infection spreads faster among them. Research has revealed that most of the users of child prostitutes are not foreigners, but this does not allow Western countries to turn a blind eye to this vile trade. Some ten countries have recently passed laws to prosecute anyone involved in paedophile activities overseas. The United States has also passed a law making it illegal to travel overseas with paedophile intentions, but in practice this law seems unworkable and no one has been prosecuted.

Developing countries are becoming more willing to co-operate in this crackdown. Previously, some were more concerned with the financial benefits of tourism, but now they are faced with the huge social and financial costs of an AIDS epidemic in their sex industry. In 1992, the Philippines introduced a new law to make it easier to prosecute paedophiles. August 1996 saw the first international conference on the exploitation of children, with more than 100 countries represented in Stockholm. Four initiatives are required to cripple this terrible industry: an international crackdown with punitive measures taken against pimps and paedophiles; job creation in developing nations to provide alternative escapes from the poverty trap; better education programmes in developing nations so that young girls and boys are encouraged to stay at school; and finally the children, most of whom are young girls, need to be rescued and taught that they have human rights and dignity – it is neither inevitable nor lawful for them to be subjugated to the will of cruel and tyrannous men. The seventh commandment is not just about the sanctity of marriage. It requires us to protect the children of the world from the deranged and depraved sexual excesses of exploitative adults.

Attitudes to adultery

Britain has been getting tougher on adulterers in politics. During the past four years, no fewer than ten Conservative MPs have been forced to resign from office as a result of their adultery being exposed in the newspapers. Even so, the Gallup morality poll of July 1996 revealed that only 47% still consider adultery wrong in all circumstances, 44% think it can occasionally be justified and 5% think it can frequently be justified. In a similar vein, as we noted previously, 47% now think that schools should not teach chastity before marriage, while 42% still want the traditional moral value preserved and taught. Roger Scruton, Professor of Philosophy at Birkbeck College, London, made an incisive valuation of these findings: 'The most important thing is the total collapse in any sexual morality – the universal acceptance of sex outside marriage and homosexual sex. Divorce rates and illegitimacy are soaring and pornographic material is widely available' (*Daily Telegraph*, Friday 5 July 1996).

The results of a similar survey in the United States provide a marked contrast. In a *Newsweek* poll, 70% say that an affair is always harmful for a marriage and only 22% say that it can sometimes be beneficial. Of those surveyed, 50% say adultery is wrong because it is immoral, 25% because it breaks up marriages and 17% because of the danger of AIDS and other diseases. Two comparative polls from the National Opinion Research Centre at the University of Chicago (NORC) are even more instructive. In 1974, a clear majority in every generation agreed that adultery is always wrong, with the smallest vote in favour among eighteen to twenty-nine-year-olds, at 59%. Twenty years later, this same generational grouping have entered mid-life, and their attitudes have hardened considerably against adultery: 74% now believe that it is always wrong. Two age groups are even more opposed to free sex: those in their sixties would be expected to represent older and more conservative values; more surprisingly, those in their twenties today are just as overwhelmingly opposed to adultery (*Newsweek*, 30 September 1996).

This dramatic shift of opinion against adultery over a twenty-year period requires a more complex explanation than the suggestion that the United States is simply more shaped by Christian values than the UK. Erica Jong, author of *The Fear of Flying* and one-time champion of sexual liberation, has repudiated the licentiousness of the seventies: 'The great experiment of my generation was that people tried to abolish jealousy. It never worked. The desire to be monogamous is more pragmatic than ethical . . . We renounced the idea of sexual freedom because it doesn't work.' The cultural experiment in sexual libertarianism has been running longer in the States, because Americans went first into the brave new world of the pill and promiscuity. A moral re-evaluation has now begun as a society faces up to the devastating consequences of adultery. Young American adults may have become more conservative because a greater number of them have had to experience the exacting price of their parents' enthusiastic dalliance with casual but costly adultery.

Royal adultery

When Charles and Diana were married, photographs of their kiss on the balcony at Buckingham Palace were reprinted in newspapers around the world. Their wedding was packaged as a royal fairy-tale and an inspiration to young love everywhere. Twenty years later, the fairy-tale in tatters, three of Queen Elizabeth's children have been married and all three are now divorced. The Windsors appear to be a typically dysfunctional modern British family. It would be gratuitous to take sides or trade in gossip, but five key factors must be recognised.

1. The Queen demanded a divorce without delay

By the beginning of 1996, the Queen's patience had evidently run out, and she feared that protracted public disputes between Charles and Diana would undermine the institution of the monarchy. Most parents would not contemplate making an intervention in their child's marriage that was quite so direct and categorical. Prince Rainier of Monaco made a similarly autocratic demand to his daughter Stephanie when her husband was photographed naked with a young model. The Prince was reported to have told Stephanie, 'Either divorce or lose your rights, your privileges and your title as princess.' It seems that Western monarchs have concluded that if they are to retain public support into the twenty-first century, they must be ruthless with adulterous in-laws in order to preserve the dignity and viability of the royal family itself.

In July 1996, the *Catholic Herald* published a strident attack on the Queen's role by William Oddie, a former Anglican priest and a leading conservative Catholic commentator. Oddie argued that the Queen had 'used her position to force divorce on a wronged wife who was anxious not to be divorced, both for the sake of the children and because she was opposed to divorce in principle . . .'. Therefore, he concluded, the Queen was in grave error, for she had repudiated the indissolubility of marriage and therefore attacked the institution of marriage itself. At the very least we must acknowledge that the Queen's assertive role has harmed her image and may well have further undermined attitudes to marriage in the nation, even though many would be sympathetic with the dilemma of any parent obliged to watch their son and his estranged wife tear one another apart in public through TV interviews.

2. Charles and Diana are both self-confessed adulterers

Both admissions came in those infamous interviews, and both were strangely incongruous, since neither had anything to gain from the admissions. Charles confessed to a liaison with Camilla Parker Bowles once his marriage had broken down, although Diana indicated in her TV interview that she thought a third party had been involved in their marriage more or less from the wedding day. Diana acknowledged her adultery with James Hewitt, who subsequently sought personal profit from selling his account of the affair. The fact of adultery on both sides is not in dispute, but neither made any public expression of repentance for their sexual indiscretions.

3. For fifty years the royal family has served as a role model to the nation

When the Queen Mother refused to leave London during the blitz, her visits to the East End became an inspiration. At the time of Charles and Diana's marriage, British newspapers anticipated a sudden increase in weddings over the next year or two, as other couples drew inspiration from the royals. It is therefore regrettably the case that others may derive a spurious legitimisation for their own divorce from the well-publicised royal behaviour: 'We might as well give up trying, just like they did.'

4. The failure of Anglican bishops to condemn royal adultery has reduced the credibility of the church

When Charles' adultery was first made public, a bishop felt obliged to comment on Radio 4. He stressed what a good job Charles was doing, and how he deserved every sympathy for a life spent under the intolerable burden of constant media attention. His comment was a royalist apologia on behalf of his monarch in waiting, but he could not bring himself to mention the simple fact that the seventh commandment condemns adultery.

The worst moment came when George Carey was interviewed by John Humphrys on the day of his speech in the House of Lords, when he would call the nation back to the Ten Commandments. Carey should have seen the question coming. Humphrys asked whether there was any connection between his imminent speech and the fact that the papers were full of the royal divorce. Carey's initial reply sounded awkward and evasive: 'Well, yes, it is quite accidental. I want to say that the Royal Family have my total support. . . . The two things must not be seen as tied together in any sense, although issues to do with faithfulness and all these things include us all, and each one of us is responsible to God.'

Humphrys pressed him: 'Should not the Archbishop be a little more forthright and say adultery is wrong?'

Carey had already declared his 'total support' for the monarchy. Now was his opportunity to provide a similarly robust affirmation of biblical morality. His response was memorably evasive: 'I don't really want to get into that.'

The Archbishop's prevarication in this interview undermined his speech in the House of Lords before it was even made. The *Sunday Telegraph* said that his inability to condemn royal adultery was typical of a church prone to 'vacillation and uncertainty' (*Sunday Telegraph*, 7 July 1996). Keith Waterhouse in the *Daily Mail* mocked the Archbishop's craven avoidance of the direct question and his absolute determination not to say anything that might cause offence. The *Mail*'s headline expressed the widespread impression that the churchman's evasiveness had made him look foolish and weak: 'Coveting? Thou art in a very grey area' (*Daily Mail*, 8 July 1996).

5. *The majority of practising Christians do not think Charles should become Supreme Governor of the Church of England*

Charles had already provoked controversy when he expressed his wish to be crowned as 'defender of faith', modifying the specifically Christian title – 'defender of *the* faith' – that had originally been given to Henry VIII by the Pope. At the time of his divorce, a Gallup poll explored church reactions to the prospect of a divorced and possibly even remarried monarch. Faced with the prospect of a divorced Supreme Governor, 76% of bishops expressed their support. Active opposition was very apparent else-where: 40% of the clergy opposed this prospect, as did 51% of retired clergy and 54% of active laity (those who had attended a service during the previous month). Among the general population, 43% stated that they did not want a divorced monarch, which reveals, ironically, that non-churchgoers are more conservative about a divorced monarch than the clergy and much more conservative than the Anglican bishops. If Charles chose to remarry, then his ascendancy would be opposed by 52% of bishops, 56% of full-time clergy and 70% of retired clergy.

In practice, the Anglican Church can do little about its Supreme Governor. If Charles is crowned King, then the unwritten constitution automatically bestows upon him the title of Supreme Governor of the Church of England. As Elaine Storkey, leading evangelical member of the General Synod, observed in a TV interview in mid-July 1996 that was widely reported in the press, this may be an embarrass-ment to the Church, indicating 'something very wrong', but the Church of England is 'saddled with him'.

The most likely way out of this embarrassment lies with Charles, but he has shown little particular sympathy with the Church of England and has never given any intimation of personal Christian faith. If he expressed repentance and regret for his adultery, amends could be made with the Church, but that seems at present the least likely prospect. Although popular opinion is presently against the prospect of his remarriage to Camilla Parker Bowles, Charles is rumoured to be determined both to be King and to marry her.

The traditional English solution would naturally be a fudge, in which Charles is crowned King and duly appointed Supreme Governor, with a discreet veil of silence drawn by the bishops over his marital infidelities. An alternative prospect, however, is that Charles relinquishes his position as Supreme Governor. During the summer of 1996, the Queen summoned the advisory council on the future of the monarchy. This group is comprised entirely of family members and no politicians or churchmen were invited to attend their consultation. As they discussed the best way to preserve the future of the monarchy, it was understood that one of the proposed 'modernisations' was to sever the link with the Anglican Church. It would be a curious irony if the Church failed to speak out against royal adultery and it was left to the royal family to recognise that their linkage with the Church had outlived its political usefulness. The Church that began its ties with the state as a result of the adulterous excesses of the divorced King Henry VIII may yet see its privileged position finally dispensed with by another adulterous and divorced king.

Beyond adultery

Given the many factors that promote promiscuity in our society, not least the royal scandals and the media's obsession with sex, we might anticipate an almost apocalyptic acceleration of adulterous liaisons. But the pattern of adultery in the United States seems to be changing in surprising ways. In the 70s, when Shere Hite analysed figures taken from a questionnaire in *Penthouse* and other adult magazines, the proportion of American men who claimed to have indulged in an affair was as high as 66%. A similar survey through *Cosmopolitan* concluded that for women it was 54%. Modern statisticians have concluded that these figures were ridiculously overstated. The readership of *Penthouse* is hardly a cross-section of American men, and only some of this group were prepared to reply to an explicit and detailed questionnaire. It is also now recognised that a proportion chose to exaggerate their own sexual prowess in their replies. By 1994, far more credible and scientific sampling techniques were employed in a NORC survey which discovered that 21.2% of men and 11% of women admitted to committing adultery at least once. The actual incidence of adultery seems to be much lower than was being suggested just a few years ago. As a result of the earlier surveys, some might even have felt a need to conform to an illusory peer pressure. They thought that 'everyone was doing it', but even in the swinging sixties, adultery was a minority leisure pursuit.

The latest research in the United States allows us to analyse the changing pattern of adultery. Within the last year, as few as 4.7% of husbands and 2.1% of wives have been unfaithful. The incidence among those who are still in their first marriage is 2.8%, but among those in a subsequent marriage 4.9% were unfaithful. The highest incidence of adultery occurs geographically in the big cities (5.9%) and the lowest in rural areas (2.6%). Those with less than high school education (4.5%) and those at the other end of the educational spectrum with graduate degrees (4.4%) are the most unfaithful, while the most faithful are those with bachelor's degrees (1.9%). Low-income (under $20,000 – 5.6%) and high-income households (over $60,000 – 3.0%) experience higher levels of adultery than middle-income families ($30–39,999 – 2.3%).

When the adultery rate is measured by gender and age group, we discover that the men most likely to be unfaithful are aged between fifty-four and sixty-three (37%), whereas the highest incidence of unfaithful women is found among those aged forty-four to fifty-three (19.9%). In every age group except one men are more likely to be unfaithful than women. Among those aged twenty-two to thirty-three, 11.7% of women had committed adultery, but only 7.1% of men. Three factors may contribute to this higher adultery rate among young women. First, they are the traditional prey of older men. Second, more young women now go out to work, so their opportunities for adulterous liaisons have increased. Third, young women may also have been influenced by the women's movement to believe that they should be emulating male promiscuity, exercising an equal right to be sexually assertive and seeking sexual conquests and fulfilment. Some women may even be acting out a kind of 'gender revenge'. In a bizarre and morally repellent escapade, a Hong Kong TV programme recently paid for a group of betrayed wives to fly to Taiwan to sleep with male prostitutes. Many other women later phoned the TV station to congratulate the women for their adulterous revenge.

The great surprise of this recent research is that the younger age groups show considerably less appetite for adultery, despite their reputation for being more sexually active than older generations. Among both men and women, the age group least likely to commit adultery are those aged twenty-two to thirty-three. In the case of men, those aged fifty-four to sixty-three are more than five times as likely to be adulterous. The astonishing implication is that modern promiscuity may have peaked between the 1960s and the 1980s. Adultery may at last have begun to go out of fashion.

Despite the impression in the media, particularly in Hollywood movies and TV soaps, that adultery is a constant obsession of the world, 92% of the French and 89% of the British have stayed faithful during the past year. Even in Denmark, long a symbol of free attitudes to sex, a 1995 survey in a women's magazine, *Alt for Damerne*, found that 97% of Danes still consider monogamy to be 'natural and moral'. In our values, modern Western culture has embarked upon an emphatic repudiation of conventional sexual morality. But in our lifestyle, it may just be that younger adults have initiated a pragmatic return to monogamy, having seen in the collapse of their parents' relationships the devastating impact of adultery and divorce. The seventh commandment speaks emphatically into the traumatic consequences of our culture's obsession with unrestrained sexual licence. Do not commit adultery – the price is far too high.

8

You shall not steal.

Deuteronomy 5:19

The Eighth Commandment
Plundering the Planet

Modern standards of honesty in Britain were tested in 1996 by the *Reader's Digest*, which left eighty wallets around the country, each containing £30. The poor were often inclined to hand in the wallet with its contents intact, including one impoverished student in Glasgow who only had £10 to spend on food that week. The better off were more likely to pocket the money as a welcome bonus. Women were found to be more honest than men: two-thirds of the women who found wallets handed them in, whereas nearly half the men kept them. The Gallup morality poll (*Daily Telegraph*, Friday 5 July 1996) revealed high standards of honesty in some circumstances: 84% said it was wrong to keep quiet about being undercharged by a corner shop; 83% said it was wrong to avoid buying a ticket on public transport; and 75% said it was wrong to steal from the taxman. While the majority still stood firm against thieving, the percentage dropped to 66% who would not stay silent when undercharged by a large chain store.

Rising crime

The rising rate of crime is never far from the headlines. Before the 1920s, fewer than 100,000 offences were recorded annually in England and Wales. By 1950 the crime rate had risen to 500,000. By 1980 it had become 2.5 million, and by mid-1993 the crime rate had reached 5.7 million. Parliament was informed in 1993 that one in three men has been convicted of a crime by the age of thirty-one. The total amount of property stolen in 1992 in Britain was estimated to be worth £3 billion. The number of robberies reported each year has risen between 1979 and 1996 by 445%, four times the overall rate of increase in the crime rate. At the same time convictions have dropped from one in four to one in eleven, while convictions for rape have fallen even more alarmingly, from one in three to one in ten. We are in the grip of a crime wave, and the Home Office has given frank admission that crime pays – the proportion of crimes resulting in a caution or conviction has been estimated to be no more than 3%.

After our house was cleared out one summer while we were on holiday, an inner-city police officer told me that the average age of burglars in London is seventeen. Most of them, he explained, are funding a drug habit, selling their stolen goods quickly in a pub or at a car boot sale. In some city districts, the exception in a street is the house that has not been burgled. It seems that thieves sometimes justify their actions by depersonalising the crime: they are not really stealing from the occupiers of the house, they explain, because the insurance company will pick up the bill. One GP told me of a petty burglar whose attitude was changed when he saw the trauma caused to a family whose belongings he had plundered. Thinking only about his own financial needs, his selfishness had resulted in a complete failure of imagination, in which he saw his house clearances as a surgical strike. Confrontation with the immense and lasting distress of his victims, their acute sense not only of material loss but of the violation of their home, resulted in one young man at least vowing never to commit burglary again. This depersonalisation of victims is characteristic not only of theft and violent crime, but also of racial and sexual injustices – taking advantage of a particular group or treating them with contempt, as if the colour of their skin or their gender made them less than fully human, and legitimate targets for exploitation and abuse.

Drug abuse

Those who distribute drugs are involved in one of the most deplorable and malevolent forms of theft, deliberately fostering addictions that rob their victims not only of their money, but their freedom, and ultimately, all too often, their lives. There were nearly 48,000 drug offences recorded in 1991, double the 1986 figure. The number of registered drug addicts was nearly 25,000 by 1992, and the number of non-registered users is presumed to be five to ten times the registered number. In 1991, 36% of teenagers had experimented with illegal drugs, and a year later this had risen to 47%. The 1991 figures for fifteen- to sixteen-year-olds were as follows: Cannabis 42%; LSD 25%; Poppers (nitrites) 22%; amphetamines 16%; and solvents 13%. Senior police officers have estimated that in recent years about half of all the criminal incidents in the Greater Manchester area have been drug related. Several recent tragedies where teenagers have died after taking a single tablet of Ecstasy have given the lie to the myth that these drugs are no more than a 'recreational stimulant'.

As rates of drug abuse and addiction continue to escalate, it seems incredible that, in September 1996, some youth centres began distributing leaflets to children as young as thirteen that set out to promote 'good trips'. The LSD leaflet advises, 'Good trips are nearly always well-planned trips.' Amphetamine use can only be commended to youngsters by a description of the good feelings they can bring: the user is no longer 'bothered by hunger, tiredness and boredom' and can enjoy being 'alert, happy, wakeful, energetic, strong'. 'Ecstasy,' another leaflet explains, condoning its use, 'has got to be taken seriously. That means with respect.' The leaflets even provide practical guidance on how to plan illegal drug use: 'Timing is important. Remember this is going to last for about eight hours and there is nothing worse than having to try and talk to people who aren't tripping when you are. This is double dodgy when the straight people are parents, friends and relatives. Imagine how it freaks parents out to come downstairs at three in the morning to find their son or daughter laughing madly at the rubber plant.'

One centre distributing these leaflets is jointly run by the YMCA and Cheshire County Council. A spokesman told the *Daily Mail* that the YMCA considered the advice centre – which also dispenses free condoms to teenagers – to be a valid use of their premises (*Daily Mail*, Friday 27 September 1996). It beggars belief that a county council and an organisation with specifically Christian origins should apparently condone such promotion of illegal and dangerous substance abuse. Since the drugs themselves are illegal, it is to be hoped that the police will be given the same power to seize such literature as they have to seize and destroy pornography. The promotion of drug abuse, by pushers or by misguided youth workers, is a form of theft that robs our children of their future liberty and life.

Thieving fathers

Those who promote illicit drugs are not the only adults to steal from children. In Britain, the Child Support Agency has attracted widespread criticism of long delays and of imposing excessive demands upon absent fathers. Despite these complaints, the CSA revealed in July 1996 that nearly 80% of single parents receive no maintenance from their former partners. Most who do receive payments get less than £50 per week from the absent parent. In the United States, it is estimated that 800,000 women and children could be removed from the welfare register if absent fathers were reliably paying child support. In July 1996, President Clinton denounced this theft by absent parents – almost always fathers – from their own children as a 'moral outrage and social disaster'. The President announced plans to have delinquent parents listed on the Internet, with their faces appearing on 'Wanted' notices at post offices. His warning was blunt: 'If you don't pay, we will track you down.' This shameful pattern of fathers stealing from their own children needs to be eradicated.

Stealing from the state

For many people, fiddling social security or an income tax return is much more palatable than failing to provide support for children. The value of the hidden 'cash in hand' economy that avoids VAT and income tax is a matter for speculation, but benefit fraud in Britain is currently estimated to be £3 billion a year. In 1995, £1.4 billion's worth of fraudulent claims was detected and refused – twice the figure for 1994. Peter Lilley, the Social Security Secretary, introduced further reforms of the system during the summer of 1996. In July it was announced that claimants of income support would not only face stricter demands to provide full information to support their claims, but they would no longer be chased up once their claim lapsed. At the beginning of August, Lilley launched the 'shop-a-benefit-cheat' phone-line, accompanied by an unsubtle sales pitch: 'Know a benefit rip-off? Give us a telephone tip-off.' A DSS official quickly dubbed the phone-line 'an extraordinary success', taking a total of 1,650 anonymous calls on the first day alone, mainly about people who were working for cash in hand while signing on. Others complained that it was a snoopers' charter, open to abuse by neighbours who bear a grudge. The phone-line is an unsavoury development that is unlikely to last: its chief contribution may prove to be not so much to catch benefit cheats as to give the impression that the government continues to be tough on crime. The government has a duty to pursue with equal vigour two kinds of theft from the state – benefit fraud, usually by the poor, and tax evasion, usually by the rich, aided and abetted by specialist tax advisers.

The least promising assaults on theft come from the hapless Serious Fraud Office, which has made a habit of prosecuting enormously long and complex court cases that cost vast sums of taxpayers' money, bamboozle juries with their financial complexity, and consistently fail to deliver a guilty verdict against the accused. The only reasonable way forward will be to take such cases out of the normal legal process, developing a specialist team of judges – and juries, if necessary – in order that the sheer complexity and high failure rate do not bring the Serious Fraud Office itself into serious disrepute.

Software theft

According to the computer industry, software theft has become endemic, not only among the large-scale pirating companies often found in China and other developing markets, but also as the casual practice of computer users across the Western world, passing duplicate copies of commercial software to their friends. Just as children pass on copies at the school gate, adults take home illegal copies of the programs used at work. Taiwanese police recently made a record seizure of pirated software as part of an aggressive crackdown designed to eradicate open abuses of international copyright law. The total value of their raids was estimated at $74 million. The software theft rate in Ireland and Germany is thought to be over 80%, and in the UK, where the rate is thought to be 40%, the cost to the industry of pirated software comes to £500 million each year.

If the software theft rate is not severely curtailed, there will be fewer companies able to continue to prosper in the computer industry, and the price of software is likely to continue to escalate. The defences of casual software piracy are all too familiar: software's too expensive to buy; everyone's doing it; I'm just testing it to see whether I want to buy my own copy; I'm sure I'll never get caught; one copy will never make a dent in the manufacturer's profits. The eighth commandment stands uncompromisingly against such specious pleading: all illicit copies are theft. What is true of computer software is equally true of the illegal copying of CDs and cassettes.

Ecological theft

In our excessive consumption of the world's non-renewable resources and our despoliation of the environment, the West is stealing the future of our planet and robbing our children's children of their inheritance. The BSE crisis has been provoked by our violation of the natural order for reasons of greed. Turning cows into carnivores, we made them unwitting devourers of their own kind. No one can yet know how widespread will be the consequent incidence of CJD, the human form of this deadly, brain-wasting disease.

The countryside is being pillaged for short-term gain. To take one small example, between 1945 and 1985, 96,000 miles of hedgerow were lost in England. Between 1984 and 1990, the rate of wanton destruction had so accelerated that we lost a further 53,000 miles. At least half these hedgerows predate the period of enclosures and as many as one in five dates back to Anglo-Saxon times. Once destroyed, the traditional face of the English countryside will never be restored. Its distinctive beauty will be lost for ever.

As to the global impact of our greed and short-termism, an international conference on climate change in Geneva in July 1996, the Intergovernmental Panel on Climate Change, comprising more than 2,000 scientists and experts, warned that human activity is likely to increase the temperature of the atmosphere by three degrees Centigrade during the next century. The results threaten to be catastrophic, bringing an increase not only in droughts but also in storms and floods as the polar ice caps begin to melt. Many coastal areas and low-lying tropical islands will be immersed as sea levels rise. John Gummer, Britain's Environment Secretary, surprised many of his critics by calling for global initiatives to achieve rapid reduction in the levels of greenhouse gases. He called for industrialised countries to cut their emissions to 10% below 1990 levels by 2010. Measures he proposed to achieve this included an increase in road fuel duties, a worldwide tax on aviation fuel, which is at present exempt from tax, and an end to subsidies that promote the use of fossil fuels, particularly oil and coal.

About half the greenhouse gases worldwide are caused by burning fossil fuels, the three main offenders being oil, coal and gas. The United States produces more greenhouse gases, including carbon dioxide, than any other country and American representatives at the Geneva conference warned that the suggested reduction of carbon dioxide emissions by 20% by 2005 was unrealistic. Sterner opposition to the greening of the global economy came from China, Kuwait, Saudi Arabia and nine other oil-producing nations. With their own short-term gains in mind, both in exporting oil and, in the case of China, the pursuit of rapid industrialisation with a casual disregard for the extremely damaging side-effects in terms of greenhouse gases and other pollution, these twelve nations bluntly declared that they did not accept the conclusions of the scientific advisory panel. The future environmental well-being of the planet is by no means certain. The creation that God considered 'very good' continues to be grievously disfigured by the rapacious plundering of its resources by the industrialised and industrialising nations.

Stealing from refugees

In March 1996, 3,145 asylum seekers came to Britain. In June, when the government had removed their right to social security benefits, the number dropped to 920. In July, after the Appeal Court decreed that the ban was unlawful, the number rose again to 1,700. The question is: Who is robbing whom? When Peter Lilley, the Social Security Secretary, introduced the new legislation in February 1996, his intention was twofold: to save the Treasury £200 million and to deter bogus asylum seekers who are motivated more by taking easy money from the British state than any genuine fear of persecution at home. Home Office Minister Timothy Kirkhope revealed that the majority of asylum seekers are already living in Britain, often as students or on short-term visas, who apply for asylum when their previous entitlement to residency is due to expire. From this perspective, the numbers speak for themselves. Britain is being robbed by specious claims for asylum.

The decision of the Appeal Court received strong backing from church leaders. The Archbishop of Canterbury, Dr George Carey, the Catholic primate Cardinal Basil Hume and Kathleen Richardson of the Free Church Federal Council wrote to *The Times* to defend a flexible and compassionate approach, while recognising that 'a substantial majority of asylum applications are rejected' (*The Times*, Monday 15 July 1996). In particular, they objected to the government's rejection of the proposed 'three-day rule', under which asylum seekers would be allowed three days within which to lodge their request for asylum, before they forfeit any eligibility to social security.

According to the government, their stricter approach – social security only available to those who seek asylum at the point of entry to Britain – discourages business people, students and tourists from subsequently changing their reasons for entering Britain and submitting a spurious request for asylum. The church leaders pointed out that any genuine refugee will need to leave their own country under some other pretext. When they arrive in Britain they may be disoriented and fearful, reluctant to change their 'official' story when speaking with immigration officers. Only when they have met up with their family and friends, and taken advice from those they trust, will some refugees feel sufficiently confident to lodge their request for asylum. From the perspective of the church leaders, three days' grace was a necessary minimum expression of compassion towards bewildered refugees.

The political debate came to an abrupt end. On Monday 15 July the government overturned the three-day amendment from the House of Lords, in a decisive vote in the Commons. Despite the views of church leaders, judges, opposition parties and some Tory MPs, Peter Lilley spoke against the amendment, warning that its implementation would cost £80 million. John McCarthy, long-term hostage in Beirut, protested against the harshness of the new policy: 'The suggestion that people who have been abused, and seen friends and relatives similarly abused and even murdered, should be capable at once of addressing bureaucratic minutiae to present a case for asylum, in an alien language, is both cruel and absurd' (quoted in *The Independent*, Tuesday 16 July 1996).

It is to be hoped that the Asylum Bill will be repealed by the next government. Of course there are those who take advantage of state support, but their appeals for asylum can be subsequently weeded out. Many fear that the present legislation, in seeking to eradicate abuses of the system, puts the exclusion of the bogus above the inclusion of the genuine. Natural justice requires that we place the higher priority upon providing a genuine opportunity of escape for refugees. As Tory backbencher Sir Julian Critchley MP observed, 'It is of course impossible to distinguish the genuine from the fraudulent until a case has been thoroughly examined' (*The Times*, Monday 15 July 1996). In its present form, the Asylum Bill is stealing the opportunity for a new life in Britain from the powerless and persecuted, whose needs by definition are always acute. The shameful consequence, at Christmas 1996, was that the Red Cross began distributing food parcels to destitute refugees in Britain.

Rich and poor

Wealth and profit should never be thought of as dirty words, and no serious political, economic or ethical analyst can seriously argue that every kind of work should receive the same rate of pay. Nonetheless, Christians accept a responsibility not only to care for the poor but also to ask why they are poor and what can be done to give them greater opportunities to enjoy the benefits of prosperity.

Two international reports in 1996 raised searching questions about acceptable levels of inequality, both within and between nations. The OECD (Organization for Economic Co-operation and Development) annual report, *Employment Outlook*, warned that Britain and the United States are the only countries where earnings inequality is rising rapidly. The percentage of the workforce in low-paid jobs is an average of 10–15% in industrialised countries, but 20% in Britain and 25% in the United States. The OECD report also reveals that these two countries also have the lowest rates of 'upward mobility' in the job market. This caused them to give a warning that 'labour market exclusion can easily turn into poverty and dependency'. The *1996 Human Development Report* from the United Nations noted that Britain and Australia are the countries with the most extreme contrasts in income between rich and poor: the richest 20% earn ten times as much as the poorest 20%. The wealth gap in the United States is only slightly smaller. The British government's own statistics confirm the emergence of a growing underclass, trapped in unemployment and poverty: 4.5 million individuals of working age lived in workless households in 1994, compared with 1.2 million in 1974.

To help the poor escape from poverty and unemployment traps, the OECD report advised that tax and benefit initiatives will be required. It also warned that too many young people leave school ill-equipped for the modern workplace. Britain in particular is facing an educational shortfall, with only 32% of young men and 38% of young women staying at school until eighteen. The OECD averages are 64% and 66%. If the impoverishment of the underclass is not addressed, we all risk becoming the losers. When an underclass feels there is no way out of poverty, no realistic employment opportunities, it begins to opt out of the normal framework of law and order, establishing private enclaves of lawlessness in the toughest of housing estates. There are already areas of public housing in the major cities of the Western world where police officers dare not walk alone. If an underclass is abandoned in their poverty as society gets richer, we simply do not know how long it might take before they consider themselves to be so alienated that they become ungovernable.

A world of extremes

The UN Development Report also revealed that the world's 358 billionaires, including the Sultan of Brunei and Bill Gates of Microsoft, possess greater wealth than the combined incomes of countries that contain 45% of the world's population. *The Independent* summed up this startling comparison with the headline, '358 billionaires who own half the world' (*Independent*, Tuesday 16 July 1996). It would be entirely specious for anyone except a doctrinaire Marxist to assert that the rich can only have prospered by taking advantage of the poor. Extreme inequality is not necessarily the direct result of injustice and exploitation. However, the rich and powerful do have a duty of care in the Judaeo-Christian tradition when faced with certain economic tendencies: extreme contrasts between the rich and the poor; the frequent inability of the poor to break out of their poverty trap unaided; and the structural inequities that produce a bias to the haves so that the rich get richer while the poor get poorer.

The only problem with Ronald Reagan's 'trickle down' theory of wealth creation, in which the poor automatically get richer as a result of the rich getting richer, was that it didn't work. Without initiatives to give the poor hope for future economic well-being, we are guilty of ignoring their plight, leaving them in their poverty trap, and robbing them of any realistic opportunity to enter into the prosperity we enjoy.

When we consider foreign debt, we turn from the responsibility to offer assistance to the poor to the obligation to recognise what has become an unjust and unworkable system of international finance. The total external debt of developing nations to the International Monetary Fund and the World Bank has grown faster than any other kind of debt. Between 1980 and 1994 it rocketed from $61 billion to $313 billion. Although at first sight this may suggest that the developing nations are the recipients of rapidly increasing Western largesse, we have to ask who the real beneficiaries are in this arrangement. As their indebtedness continues to grow, developing countries have been burdened with an absurd obligation to pay back even larger sums than they receive in aid from the West, in order to service the interest on loans from the Western banking system.

It would be naïve in the extreme to suggest that all abuses of the system are one-sided. In one notorious incident in 1983, Zaïre had to respond to IMF demands to make sweeping budget cuts. The Zaïrian solution was to fire one-third of the nation's civil servants and teachers, including several thousand fictitious state employees. Some headteachers decided to retain their fictitious staff, pocketing the salaries paid in their names, while removing real teachers. Endemic corruption in the nation exacerbated the already severe consequences of the IMF budgetary strategy.

The US Treasury has acknowledged that the present system certainly benefits the American economy: 'Last year, more than $2.7 billion went to US firms that had won contracts to help carry out projects and programs funded through development banks. This figure was nearly twice the $1.5 billion the US paid into the banks for that year. It gave us an export bonus of nearly 80%' (*The Multilateral Development Banks*, May 1994). Britain enjoys a similar economic advantage, for the only continent where Britain has a trade surplus in manufactured goods is Africa, and Africa is also the continent most indebted to British loans. The subtitle of the American Treasury report shows great candour in spelling out the advantages to the United States in supporting the IMF, the World Bank and other development banks: '*increasing US exports and creating US jobs*'. This would be no more than a frank acknowledgement of enlightened self-interest if the arrangement was also to the advantage of the developing nations. But this is not the case.

Eighty-nine countries, mainly in sub-Saharan Africa, have lower per capita incomes than ten years ago. Nineteen countries, including Rwanda, Sudan, Ghana, Venezuela and Haiti, actually have per capita incomes today that are lower than they were in 1960. As a percentage of average American earnings, Brazilians earn 12.1%, Jamaicans 5%, Haitians 1.9%, Zaïrians 1.2% and Nepalis 0.9%. James Speth, administrator for the United Nations Development Programme, gave a stark warning: 'The world has become more economically polarised. If present trends continue, economic disparities between industrial and developing nations will move from inequitable to inhuman.'

Increasing indebtedness leads to a situation where it is

inconceivable that many developing nations will ever be able to clear their overseas loans. Their extreme indebtedness has also obliged them to employ economic strategies imposed by the IMF, and this often entails increasing their production of commodities for sale overseas, such as coffee, tea, cocoa, sugar and timber. However, the economic law of supply and demand means that if a number of developing nations increase production of the same crops, their value on the world market declines. As a result, a developing nation may be caught in the double bind of producing more and earning less, while simultaneously facing an escalating debt mountain as compound interest continues to accrue. At the same time, debt servicing becomes a more immediate priority than addressing the problems of health, water provision and education. As Dr Jeffrey Sachs, one of the key contributors to strategies for the economic regeneration of post-communist Eastern Europe, has observed of the role of the IMF, the World Bank and the regional development banks: ' . . . while these institutions have been discouragingly ineffectual in Africa, they still have the leading role in Western advice and assistance to the African nations' (*Understanding Shock Therapy*, published by the Social Market Foundation, 1994).

The injustice of international aid and debt is plain. The donor countries enjoy additional prosperity as a result of their contributions, while the debtor countries fall further into debt. Under a veneer of altruism and with frequent complaints that the developing nations are failing to manage their economies properly, the rich are getting richer at the expense of the poor. Many have concluded that the iron grip of indebtedness amounts to nothing less than economic slavery. Just as children in Pakistan are handed over to work as bondslaves, often for example in carpet factories, when their parents are unable to repay a loan, the entire population of developing nations has been placed in economic bondage to the West. This economic bondage is nothing less than stealing from the poor for the benefit of the rich.

Under the present system there is no realistic prospect of escape. The loans and the interest upon them are rising faster than the capacity to pay, while the underlying issues of health, education and building an economic infrastructure fail to receive the attention and expenditure they require. The 1995 OXFAM Poverty Report noted, '35,000 children die every day from diseases which could be prevented through access to adequate nutrition and the most basic health provision.' In 1970 100 million people in sub-Saharan Africa went hungry. Despite the fivefold increase in loans from the IMF and World Bank in the last fifteen years, by 2010 the number who are hungry is projected to increase to an even more devastating 300 million (*International Herald Tribune* editorial, 16 March 1995).

Kenneth Clarke, the Chancellor of the Exchequer, has proposed an imaginative solution for the top twenty developing countries who have begun to implement successful economic reforms but are still faced with enormous debts to the IMF and the World Bank. On 29 September 1996, the Interim Committee of the IMF agreed to implement two new initiatives. The Clarke plan will provide $6 billion of debt relief to these countries. At the same time, the 'Paris Club' that represents the export credit agencies of the main industrialised nations will write off as much as 80% of the debts of countries qualifying for the IMF debt relief initiative. In order to finance the plan, the IMF is expected to sell five million ounces of gold, generating about $2 billion, despite objections from Germany. Mr Clarke has stated that he anticipates that these new funds will become available before the end of 1996 and Uganda is expected to be the first beneficiary. For the more successful developing economies, the Clarke initiative is a major step towards complete liberation from the debt trap. As Perez de Cuellar, former UN Secretary General, has stated, 'We are clearly witnessing what is probably an irresistible shift in public attitudes towards the belief that the defence of the oppressed in the name of morality should prevail over frontiers and legal documents' (quoted in *Pennies from Seven*, Christian Aid, 1995).

The Clarke plan addresses the needs of countries making promising progress, but Christian Aid estimates that there may be twenty to thirty-five countries that are facing severe long-term difficulties (*Pennies from Seven*, Christian Aid, 1995). The most imaginative solution for the poorest of countries to escape from this intractable inequity has been produced by Jubilee 2000, who have gone much further than Mr Clarke in calling for a one-off remission of *unpayable* debts before the year 2000. The objections are predictable. It would be unworkable, threatening the entire system of international banking, setting an extremely dangerous precedent, and establishing an economic climate in which other countries would default on their loans. The cry of the poor and the eighth commandment both demand to be heard. We have been fleecing the poor to enrich the rich, and the international repudiation of this wretched injustice is long overdue.

We have ranged widely in this chapter, from personal integrity to the crime rate, from absent fathers to drug abuse, from software piracy to greenhouse gases, from protecting refugees to the world debt crisis. The eighth commandment stands against all kinds of theft, from personal to international. It is not a command that can be squeezed into a narrow political agenda of the left or the right. Like all the commandments it asks probing questions of every political perspective, for it prompts us to defend law and order, protect personal property and yet to speak out for the needs of the weak and the poor. If we had the courage and conviction to apply the eighth commandment comprehensively, we would have the opportunity to experience a safer and fairer society and world.

9

You shall not give false testimony
against your neighbour.

Deuteronomy 5:20

The Ninth Commandment

A Culture of Duplicity

The senior British civil servant explained patiently to the Australian court that he had not been lying. He had merely been 'economical with the truth'. It is rarely that a civil servant's words enter common currency, but this phrase has stuck. The popular British TV series, *Yes Prime Minister*, provided a devastatingly witty account of the verbal subterfuge and evasiveness of the mandarins of government, in which the unthinkable act was for Sir Humphrey ever to give a straight answer. Suddenly the real world out Sir Humphreyed the TV programme. The credibility of the public life of the nation was eroded another notch.

Deceit in politics

The convention of the British parliament has long been that you cannot call another MP a liar – although Churchill once infamously evaded this restriction by speaking of a 'terminological inexactitude'. However, every campaign trail has come to be littered with gross caricatures of the opposition and promises that are always broken. In the eighties, after decades in which politicians had habitually promised what proved to be unattainable levels of employment and prosperity, both American Republicans and British Conservatives began to emphasise the virtues of a minimalist government. George Bush promised 'no new taxes'. When the striking sound-bite became a broken promise, it was a quote that came back to haunt him. Mrs Thatcher and her shadow Chancellor promised there would be no increases in Value Added Tax. When they came to office VAT stood at 8% and by the time she reluctantly departed it was 17.5%. The iron lady shared with Ronald Reagan a teflon quality that kept her in office, despite the broken promises. Like George Bush, John Major seems to be the hapless successor left to pick up the tab.

Duplicity is not only endemic in election promises but in the processes of parliamentary debate. The sheer artificiality of a two-party system squeezes every debate into the simplistic confrontation of two opposing perspectives. There is little room either to acknowledge the complexity of an issue or to work for an all-party consensus. Whatever is good in the country is claimed by the government as a direct result of their astute leadership; whatever is bad is laid at their door by the opposition. No one in office is prepared to say, 'We made a mistake.' No one in opposition is prepared to say, 'It's such a complex issue, we have no answers either. It's really not the government's fault.' Prime Minister's Question Time is not so much serious political debate as a gratuitously macho, rumbustious knockabout. Combative rhetorical virtuosity is preferred to intelligent and reasoned argument. There is a singular lack of credibility on both sides.

Politicians are almost invariably unpopular, but they sink still further in public esteem when they vote themselves massive pay increases. In July 1996, British MPs gave themselves a huge 26% pay increase, in a year when the government was offering public sector workers just one-tenth as much. The Prime Minister's pay promptly went up from £84,217 to £143,000. Backbench MPs' pay rose to £43,000, plus office allowances amounting to a further

£42,754. Despite public calls for restraint from all the party leaders, MPs voted overwhelmingly for these increases, provoking considerable debate as to whether their salaries had fallen behind or whether they were just being greedy ahead of the election. Self-interest brought the backbenchers flocking into the lobbies together: Tory MPs who expected to lose their seats qualified for post-election payments related to this higher salary, while Labour MPs secured the pay rises under a Tory government, avoiding embarrassment for the anticipated incoming Labour administration.

One aspect of this pay increase remained almost hidden from view, for the Commons subsequently agreed to cut MPs' mileage allowance from 74p per mile for larger cars to 47p. Some MPs had previously stated that if the pay increase was not secured, they would insist on retaining the higher rate of travel allowance. There was only one explanation for this extraordinarily high mileage rebate. In order to postpone the public unpopularity that follows a large pay increase, MPs had previously given themselves a backdoor bonus through artificially inflated travelling expenses. What this represents is an institutionalisation of deceit against the taxpayer. Every time an MP had filled in an expenses claim under the previous system, the principle of integrity in public life had been compromised.

For civil servants, the most delicate issue is the need to avoid telling lies to parliament. Many answers to parliamentary questions, both verbal and written, are polished masterpieces of ambiguity. The apparent meaning will frequently give reassurance to the inexperienced questioner, while the real truth is concealed between the lines. Upon such linguistic niceties a government minister may stand or fall. When the language of government demonstrates continual excesses of evasiveness, while civil servants and cabinet ministers may not be technically lying, they have undoubtedly made a profession out of providing calculated misinformation to the House and the media.

In the United States, deceit similarly appears to be endemic in public life. For example, an investigation was launched in July 1996 into charges that immigration officials may have been under orders not to report all the arrests made near the border with Mexico. The apparent intention of this alleged policy of deceit was to convey the impression that the Clinton adminstration's high-profile $30 million initiative to reduce illegal immigration from Mexico had been a resounding success. Any attempt to falsify arrest reports and intelligence records for the sake of political gain is a fundamental violation of the integrity of law enforcement and public office.

Deceit and the military

It's not just politics that is soured by deceit. The ninth commandment is ever more widely 'more honoured in the breach than in the observance'. In the Gulf War, Western TV screens were filled with two kinds of triumph: the smart bombs that made precision hits in Iraq, and the Patriot missiles that made light work of the Iraqis' Scud missile attacks on Saudi Arabia and Israel. Only after the war was long over did the truth begin to come out. The smart missiles were not all that smart. Some did not hit the intended targets at all; others accurately hit targets that proved not to be strategic military centres after all. A smart bomb is only as bright as the information with which it is programmed. Worse, the immense cost of these missiles has now led some Pentagon advisers to suggest that they are strategically inferior to conventional weapons. As to the Patriots, the CNN bulletins were repeated on many TV stations worldwide, along with the official military explanation that the Scud missiles were picked off in their entirety. In due course it became apparent that the Patriots' success was much more patchy. The exaggerated reports about both kinds of missiles were used to win the propaganda war. The tales about smart bombs reassured the public in the West that our attacks were discriminate, targeting only the military. The apparent precision of the Patriot missiles created a myth of impregnability for any city or country protected by the latest Western technology. The old principle of waging war has not changed: the first casualty is always truth.

To expose Western propaganda is by no means to exonerate Saddam Hussein. When the former head of Iraqi military intelligence, General Wafiq al-Sammara'i, defected, he claimed that Saddam was continuing to lie about his chemical weapons. Since the Gulf War, the United Nations has been trying to destroy all Iraqi missiles and stores of toxic agents, including botulinus and anthrax. The head of the UN monitoring team, Rolf Elkeus, was already persuaded that Iraq might be concealing 'six to sixteen missiles with long-range capability'. Now General Sammara'i has warned that Saddam has hidden as many as '40 missiles and 255 containers of biological and chemical weapons' (*Independent*, Friday 5 July 1996). Such deception could enable Saddam to secure the lifting of UN sanctions, while retaining the firepower to establish military domination in the region.

Deceit in business

Once upon a time, an Englishman's word was his bond. Now when he promises that the cheque is in the post, you had better not rely on it until it has arrived. Even then it might bounce. When John Major spoke out against the deception of paying bills late, a millionaire member of his party revealed that his own wealth had been built up by just such a policy of deferred payments.

The Scott Report into the arms to Iraq scandal exposed

the fact that British politicians had been involved in the covert encouragement of British companies to exploit loopholes in regulations restricting overseas trade. Officially, the national interest required trade restrictions. Out of the public eye, it seemed that leading members of the government took the view that there was a higher national interest in maximising all possible trade opportunities, even with Saddam Hussein.

Yorkshire Water has been widely criticised for its handling of the water shortage since the summer of 1995, when the supply of water to many homes was intermittent or cut off. One leading executive made extravagant claims on TV about no longer taking regular showers that were later exploded by the press. In July 1996, Yorkshire Water was seeking leave from an enquiry inspector to continue to enforce a drought order and to take additional supplies from the River Hull. To do this, they had to submit figures for the amount of rain that had fallen at the Langsett Rain Gorge in South Yorkshire in September 1995. The Environment Agency figure was 130.4 millimetres. The figure submitted by Yorkshire Water was 100.4 millimetres. *The Daily Telegraph* revealed that Yorkshire Water had admitted changing the rainfall figure, on the basis that it was a 'freak result' (*Daily Telegraph*, Wednesday 10 July 1996). It was, of course, considerably to the advantage of their appeal to the drought enquiry to suggest that 25% less rain had fallen than was really the case.

Another of the major utilities privatised in recent years is British Gas, sold off from government ownership in 1986. It was a flagship privatisation, for which the advertising centred on 'Sid', the ordinary man in the street who was invited to benefit from becoming a shareholder. At the time, many thousands of 'Sids' took up the invitation expectantly. Sir Dennis Rooke, Chairman of British Gas from 1976 to 1989, chose the day in July 1996 that nuclear energy shares began trading on the stock exchange to denounce the government's handling of his old business and its shareholders. He complained that when the company was sold, British Gas was the sole supplier to domestic customers, but this and many other trading arrangements have since been changed. The shares Sid bought in British Gas have produced a poor yield, due to growing uncertainty about the future of the company. In ten years, their capital return has been 40%, whereas the index of Britain's top 100 companies shows a return over the same period of 164%. In an interview for BBC's *Nine o'Clock News*, Sir Dennis' criticism was blunt: 'Over the years "Sid" certainly has been conned.'

Early in the BSE crisis, in 1989 the British government banned the use of meat and bone meal made from cow and sheep remnants in any feed manufactured for cattle. Rather than abandoning a method of maximising profits that was now thought to produce a devastating disease, British companies promptly increased their exports to France, Germany and Israel. In the year this kind of cattle feed was banned in Britain, we doubled our exports. The UK Renderers' Association insisted they had 'applied whatever legislative controls the government introduced'. But someone had seen a loophole, so a dangerous feed, illegal in the country of manufacture, was hastily shipped overseas without mentioning the hazards to the farmers in those countries. Tragically, but unmistakably, a culture of duplicity has come to pervade much of the business community today.

In the United States, the trial of a Wall Street financier that began in September 1996 could result in him facing a total sentence of 165 years in jail. Christopher Bagdasarian began investing at the age of eleven and by nineteen he was worth $40 million. At thirty-one he now faces charges of an alleged confidence trick in which banks were persuaded to support a $200 million public share offer for his reinsurance company, on the basis of false financial statements. They were persuaded to back him, following claims that he provided investors with average returns of 29% and that his personal worth was $500 million. His borrowings included $24 million used to purchase a personal jet and a $6 million estate. Paul Gerlach of the US Securities Exchange Commission said: 'We investigate a lot of fraud and I haven't seen a fraud as audacious as this. I guess the notion is that if you tell a big enough lie, nobody's going to challenge it.'

Deceit and the media

The tabloid press are renowned for several kinds of frequent false witness. Sensational front page headlines sell newspapers, but may grievously distort the real story. Quotations are deliberately taken out of context to misrepresent a viewpoint, or may even be entirely fabricated. Stories are concocted that are pure fiction. Rumour, gossip and innuendo are repeated so often that the distinction between truth and fiction is seriously blurred. Personal privacy is now routinely invaded, with photos shot through long-distance telephoto lenses and the recording of mobile phone conversations. All too often the resultant story is more concerned with sensation than truth. If newspapers were divided into three sections – facts, comment and falsehood – the third section would be by far the largest in the British and American tabloid press.

Serious current affairs programmes on TV and radio are faced with their own crisis of false witness, for the sound-bite has replaced reasoned argument as the approved mode of discourse. Despite the apparent antagonism of searching questions and robust responses, journalists and politicians take part in a mutually beneficial, symbiotic relationship. Idealistic journalists may see themselves as pursuers of truth, but if they want to stay on air they must also chase the ratings. An aggressive style not only combats the politician's habitual evasiveness, but the journalist must also interrupt any long-winded answer that viewers may find too boring. At the same time, politicians not only want to avoid the difficult question, they also want to insert a sound-bite they prepared earlier. It really doesn't matter what question the interviewer asks – only the thirty-second snippet will be replayed on the news and fill the headlines in the next morning's papers. Candour and clarity are early victims of the quest for popularity which some politicians and journalists appear to have made a tacit common cause.

In Italy, TV sleaze has plumbed new depths. One programme, *Telecamere a Richieste – TV Cameras on Request* – which has been described by *The Independent* as 'particularly squalid', secretly films men who are shortly to be married being seduced by women who are testing their faithfulness in the name of TV entertainment (*Independent*, Monday 22 July 1996). Entrapment for the sake of ratings is a blatant and totally unjustifiable kind of deceit. The most famous Italian presenter, Pippo Baudo, has been the target of several allegations: that he rigged a New Year lottery draw broadcast live on TV; that he promoted personal friends who took part in talent contests; and that he allowed himself to be bribed when picking contestants for the 1996 San Remo music festival. Scantily clad young women adorn many shows in Italy, and allegations are also being investigated that these girls are told that the pathway to a successful career in TV is to sleep with agents, producers and TV personalities. Politicians with an interest in TV have also allegedly been bribed by being offered time with some of the aspiring starlets. Many young girls have apparently agreed to dispense sexual favours only to be dumped and forgotten. In Italian TV it seems that deceit abounds both on and off screen.

Deceit and sport

The most famous goal ever scored by Diego Maradonna was against England in the World Cup. The ball was crossed too high for the athletic but short Argentinian, who promptly stuck out a hand and palmed the ball into the net. To the fury of the English team, the referee and linesman failed to see the foul and Maradonna celebrated a goal that should never have been. The most brilliant footballer of his generation was seen by millions to be a cheat. This infamous handball was not Maradonna's only moment of deceit. Among drug charges later brought against him was the accusation that he had taken ephedrine, a banned stimulant, during the 1994 World Cup.

The most notorious drug abusing sportsman of recent years is undoubtedly Ben Johnson of Canada, stripped of the 100 metres gold medal for using the steroid stanozolol at the 1988 Olympic Games. Johnson's cheating continues to devalue the achievements of today's top athletes. Whenever someone achieves a record-breaking triumph, there is always a nagging suspicion that they may have been aided by performance enhancing drugs. Chris Brasher, Olympic steeplechase gold medallist for Britain in 1956, gave voice to this growing sense of disillusionment when he announced that he would be boycotting the 1996 Olympics, the first he had missed for forty years. His explanation was simple: 'It's the pressure to win which leads to drug taking' (*The Times*, Thursday 8 July 1996). Others point to the enormous amounts of money that can be earned by top athletes, now the old restrictions of amateurism have been abandoned, as a beguiling enticement to cheat.

China has taken over the mantle from East Germany as the country most likely to place its top athletes on a regime of illegal drugs. In the World Swimming Championships in Rome in 1994, Chinese women won twelve of sixteen events and their credibility with fellow competitors hit rock bottom. Although the international governing body tried to moderate the proposals, more than 100 swimming nations agreed in 1996 to a strict regime of punishments for drug cheats. One offence will mean a four-year suspension, and a second will result in an automatic life ban. If four swimmers from any one nation have positive tests within any twelve-month period, the entire national team will be banned for two years.

The drugs scandal attained further notoriety shortly before the 1996 Atlanta Olympics, when Dr Michael Turner, former British Olympic team doctor, expressed his fear that over 50% of athletes have cheated by using illegal drugs. In the power events of shot, discus, javelin and sprinting, he suggested it could be as high as 75%. Two years earlier, Prince Alexandre de Merode, chair of the International Olympic Committee (IOC) medical commission, had estimated that half of all Olympic athletes now take performance enhancing drugs. The IOC are doing all they can to combat this deceit. The latest high resolution mass spectrometers that were used at the Olympics in Atlanta were installed in all accredited IOC laboratories around the world by September 1996. They are three times more sensitive than the old equipment and can detect steroids up to three months after they have been used. Maradonna's ephedrine and Johnson's stanozolol would no longer have a chance of escaping detection.

It seems that the determined drug cheats can always remain one step ahead of the equipment. While the cheaper performance enhancing drugs can now more easily be discovered, the latest drugs are not yet traceable, including the latest synthetic growth hormones. It has been claimed that the élite athletes who are able to pay up to $10,000 for a short course of drugs can guarantee that their deceit is beyond detection (*Daily Mail*, Wednesday 17 July 1996). For the moment, the deceit of performance enhancing drugs has cast a terrible shadow, not only over the future health of the drug abusers, but over the credibility of international sport.

Deceit and whistle-blowers

It has become customary in Britain for the occasional indignant nurse or doctor to speak out against the waiting lists and the failings in patient care at their hospital. The price of honesty can be their job, since an increasing number of employment contracts incorporate a clause forbidding any talk with the media. The public interest that the whistle-blower seeks to defend contravenes the interest of their employer to maintain a positive public image.

Extremely extensive – some would say repressive – restrictions are imposed upon those required to sign the British Official Secrets Act. Although the intention of the act is to protect the national interest, a veil of secrecy is cast across the entire spectrum of the affairs of government. As a result, if a whistle-blower ever speaks out against governmental corruption or deceit, they are likely to face trial under this act. As the Clive Ponting case demonstrated, when he leaked some documents that revealed governmental duplicity over the sinking of the General Belgrano, the government of the day will argue that its interests and the interests of the state are one and the same. Ponting's successful defence argued that national interest may require a duty of public disclosure, notwithstanding the political furore this may provoke. Many politicians and constitutionalists now recognise that the Official Secrets Act is a Draconian measure, obliging civil servants to keep concealed information that the public have a right to know. Sir Winston Churchill once observed: 'The Official Secrets Act was devised to protect the national defences and ought not to be used . . . to shield ministers who have strong personal interests in concealing the truth. . . .' Sir David Steel has warned, 'The level of secrecy in Britain today has reached proportions that seriously undermine the health of our democracy.'

There is a growing body of opinion that argues that

Britain needs a Freedom of Information Act and a written constitution. The deceptions of Richard Nixon and the Watergate scandal quickly became notorious worldwide. And yet it is a great tribute to the American Constitution that presidential duplicity was unmasked, forcing his resignation. If Nixon had been in power in Britain, the Official Secrets Act would have concealed his corruption and led to the prosecution of any who attempted to make public revelations.

The price of deceit

A culture of duplicity exacts a high price. Politicians, journalists and estate agents are widely held in the lowest regard, ranking at the bottom of league tables for professions that command public respect. It is taken for granted that a politician will not give a straight answer and that a party political broadcast is the lowest form of advertising. In such a climate of habitual duplicity, in government and media, business and sport, it is hardly surprising that deceit has become a casual part of everyday life. The July 1996 Gallup morality poll discovered that 10% have lied to the taxman and 30% to their husband or wife. Psychological testing of almost 1,000 British people in 1996 revealed that a side-effect of the women's movement is that young women are now not only more aggressive and arrogant – emulating these 'qualities' in young men – but also more dishonest. The familiarity of deceit in public life makes it ever easier to lie in private without qualm or scruple.

The consequences of ignoring the ninth commandment are profound. In a society where speaking only the truth is a principle that has been widely discarded, the inevitable result is a rising tide of distrust and cynicism. To recover this biblical absolute would be the first step to restoring integrity and credibility in private and public life.

10

You shall not covet
your neighbour's wife.
You shall not set your desire on
your neighbour's house or land,
his manservant or maidservant,
his ox or donkey,
or anything that belongs to your neighbour.

Deuteronomy 5:21

The Tenth Commandment
Excesses of Consumerism

In September 1996 the assets were seized of a company selling software that claimed to guarantee a profit from betting on horse racing. The program was said to guarantee winners, so that anyone who made an initial investment of £500 could expect a return within a year of no less than £43,358. In practice, the punters made a loss. The company help-line blamed unusually soft ground at the race tracks. The Department of Trade and Industry required that the firm should be wound up in the public interest. The company took £2.8 million in sales of the software, with up to forty people buying the program each week in the hope of getting rich quick. The judge, Mr Justice Carnwath, rejected the plea that it was not right for a liquidator to be called in to close a profitable company, concluding that the basis of commercial success was dependence on a lie. The greedy and the gullible had kept the company afloat.

We truly have become the acquisitive society, and money certainly does make our world go around. Fergie, the former wife of Prince Andrew, has adopted a new mantra, according to *The Times*, that has less to do with New Age versions of Buddhism than with assertive Western consumerism. One of her gurus is said to have instructed her to repeat no fewer than twenty-two times a day the following mantra of materialism: 'Money now comes to me in abundance in perfect ways.'

The early adverts for one of the major credit cards summed up our societal priority: 'Access takes the waiting out of wanting.' If you want something, the world of easy credit urges, buy it immediately, and have no regrets until the bill arrives in the post several weeks later. As we move towards a cashless society, credit facilities are available in almost every store, usually charging excessive interest rates for late payments. Those who have had to provide support for those caught in the spiral of spending money they have not earned know how easy it is for people to end up paying off one credit card with another, stacking up debts of ever-increasing magnitude. Bertrand Russell had an entirely different perspective when he warned, 'It is preoccupation with possessions, more than anything else, that prevents men from living freely and nobly.'

Advertising and marketing are the great engine room of acquisitiveness. Advertising has the threefold task of informing, combating alternative products and persuading the consumer. 'I want' must be transformed into 'I need'. It is even better if parents can be persuaded that their beloved offspring are perceived to be the chief beneficiaries of consumerism. The rationalisation is all too familiar: 'I'm not materialistic myself, but my children simply must have £80 trainers or they won't fit in at school.' Children become a pretext for adult consumerism and are trained in covetousness from an early age.

One of the most deplorable trends in modern advertising is the acute seductive pressure applied to children left alone to watch kids' TV. The toys advertised usually have a high retail price – 'only £40' – which has the intended result in many homes of increasing the parents' budget for Christmas presents. The aggressive merchandising of plastic models related to many top cartoon series means that the programmes themselves have become nothing more than an extended promotional campaign. The old dictum of the Jesuits has been given a new twist: give the advertisers a modern child before they are ten, and they will give you a dedicated consumer for life. 'But Mum, all my friends have got one of these already, so I've got to have one too.'

In politics, the power of covetousness is unmistakable. On 1 October 1996, the cash for questions scandal finally reached a sudden and unexpected conclusion, when the MP who had been exposed by *The Guardian* withdrew his libel case at the last minute. The following day *The Guardian* not only printed the evidence against this particular MP, but also presented charges and evidence that a further four Tories had been caught up in sleaze. The newspaper expressed contempt for the politician with an unequivocal front page headline: 'A Cheat and a Liar'. The love of money is not only the root of all evil, as the New Testament warns, but in the nineties it may also apparently buy an MP's advocacy for your cause in parliament. Sleaze scandals reach beyond any particular MP and party, for the reputation of Parliament itself and the credibility of all politicians is being tarnished and diminished. There is an urgent need for greater openness and tighter controls on MPs' personal and campaign funding.

In general elections, nothing so concentrates the mind of the public as the prospect of a tax cut. The Kinnock-led Labour party had a comfortable lead over John Major's Conservatives going into a general election, but it evaporated when the middle classes faced up to the startling contrasts in fiscal policy. Tony Blair and Gordon Brown have since devoted a great deal of energy to reassuring the voters that anyone earning less than £100,000 per annum will not pay higher taxes under Labour. In an age of covetousness, it has become impossible to sell the old socialist ideal of choosing to pay more tax for the sake of the poor. In opinion polls, widespread support is almost invariably expressed for higher public spending on health and education. But for most people in the voting booth, the most decisive factor is their projected personal tax bill if they vote for a particular party.

Sexual coveting

When this commandment refers to coveting someone else's wife, is this no more than undiluted, old-fashioned chauvinism? In reality, unrestrained lust all too often treats the opposite sex as mere objects of desire. Men in particular are frequently capable of depersonalising women, whether in dirty jokes, porn magazines, or gawping at a beautiful passer-by. The very language of lust reduces women to sex objects – '*That's* a nice pair of legs. . . .'

The world did not waste any tears mourning the passing of Nicu Ceausescu, son of Nicolae, the former dictator of Romania, who died aged forty-five in 1996 as a result of alcoholism. As tyrannical as his father, Nicu had been sent to prison for twenty years after the collapse of his father's dictatorship, on a charge of genocide, brought against him because the troops had opened fire in Sibiu, the city he had governed in 1989, killing at least eighty-nine and injuring some 280. Two years after his trial he was released on health grounds and then cynically pardoned by the new, crypto-communist government, along with all the other henchmen of the old regime. In his days of power, Nicu had appointed agents in the local factories to procure girls for one night stands.

During this same period, Nadia Comaneci was entrancing the world with her exquisitely elegant and beautiful gymnastic prowess, winning a gold medal for Romania at the Montreal Olympics. According to her mother, Stephania Comaneci, Nicu commanded her to attend one of his parties and savagely raped her when she was just seventeen and a virgin. No one dared complain, or Nicu would have had them shot. Subsequently, whenever Nicu coveted

Nadia, secret police would come to pick her up and she would eventually be returned home bruised and scratched. Nicu and his fellow thugs even played cards on Nadia's naked body. When she failed in an attempted defection to the United States while on a gymnastics tour, Nicu personally tore out two of her fingernails. Stephania described her unwilling but powerless daughter as 'Nicu's sex slave'.

That in all its repugnant horror is what it means to covet a woman, stripping her of all dignity and treating her with utter contempt as an object to satisfy brute desire. Lap dancing, strippers, prostitution and pornography are all expressions of sexual covetousness, reducing a woman to an object of sexual desire, bought with money or dominated by violence and power.

Coveting and the lottery

The lottery has been an enormous popular success, generating far greater turnover and profits than anyone had anticipated. In the first year, the lottery generated £1 billion for the Treasury and £1 billion for charities, with enormous profits for Camelot, currently running at £1.5 million a week. Each week £85 million is spent on tickets, and more than 100 punters became millionaires within the first year. Ticket sales in the year to March 1996 exceeded £5.6 billion, making the lottery bigger than the confectionery market (£4.5 billion). A British Academy of Sport will be launched with £100 million of lottery money, £500 million will be used to transform Britain's museums during the next four years and a further £3.2 million will be used to rebuild and renovate the Royal Exchange Theatre in Manchester, blown up by the IRA in June 1996. If the lottery is so resoundingly popular, why are voices raised against it? Nine objections still need to be made about the lottery, particularly in its present form.

1. The lottery appeals to the gullible

Two out of three British adults bet on the lottery each week, lapping up the fond hope that they could be the next to get rich quick. Their chances of a big win are minuscule. You are more likely to die on a Saturday night than win the lottery; more likely to be run over on the way to buy a ticket than to choose the jackpot numbers.

2. The lottery provokes greed

Mrs Thatcher opposed the introduction of a state lottery during her time in power, because she thought that the government should not encourage gambling. Every Saturday night the lottery programme is a national orgy of covetousness, legitimising and provoking an obsessive lust for vast, unearned wealth.

3. The lottery is a disguised tax

Income is generated for the government which is not only used to pay for previously unfunded projects, but also to finance initiatives previously paid for out of the taxation system. There is widespread suspicion that in a few years' time the lottery will be the only source of state funding for the arts, sport and charitable work.

4. The lottery discourages saving

Spend before you earn is the lifestyle of an economy built on easy credit. But this approach promotes personal irresponsibility and increases inflationary pressures. With a commitment to establishing a low or even zero inflation economy, the government should be promoting deferred rather than instant gratification. Saving invariably produces a sounder economy than gambling.

5. *The lottery overstates its charitable contributions*

A tiny percentage of lottery revenue is directed into charities, but whenever a lottery spokesperson defends Camelot's vast profits, we are invariably reminded that the success of the lottery has raised money for charities. This is a deliberate distortion of the intentions of the lottery, for the organising company's primary objective is not to raise money for charity but to maximise its own profits. Similarly, the real motivation behind buying a lottery ticket is not the desire to make a charitable donation, but the hope of personal gain. The actual impact of the lottery, according to many charities, has been to divert money away from good causes. In the past, many people were quite prepared to hand over their loose change to charities, feeding it into collecting tins on the high street. Now the income from street collections is in decline, as people keep a firmer grip on their money, preferring to use it for yet more lottery tickets. The over-emphasis on the charitable benefits paints an unconvincing veneer of generosity on a business built on greed. If people really want to give to charities, they should cut out the middlemen (Camelot's profits and the Treasury) and make a direct donation.

6. *The lottery has brought 'pork-barrel politics' to Britain*

In the States, pork-barrel politics is all too familiar, with politicians making the maximum political capital out of state expenditure in order to win – or buy – votes. Although the British government has deliberately distanced itself from the decision-making process on how to spend lottery money, leading politicians are often involved in the announcement of funding and the opening of projects supported by the lottery. Lord Archer, former MP, bestselling novelist and irrepressible party enthusiast, believes that every Tory MP should always have in his pocket a list of lottery financed projects in his constituency and that its positive impact should be talked about constantly: 'It wouldn't have happened without this government and it is a triumph for the Conservatives' (quoted in *The Sunday Times*, 4 August 1996).

7. The benefits of the lottery are trivial compared with the enormous publicity

In its first twenty-one months, grants from the lottery amounted to £2 billion. The social security budget almost matches this sum every single week. The enormous visibility of lottery funded spending has a political impact, promoting the feel-good factor. It also serves as free advertising on behalf of Camelot, encouraging the public to buy more tickets, not only for the sake of personal gain and the charities, but also to contribute to the general well-being of the nation.

8. The lottery targets the poor

Those with least chance of earning a good income are often the most easily seduced with promises of instant wealth. The percentage of income devoted to lottery tickets is highest among the poor. However, many of the major projects sponsored by the lottery, such as the redevelopment of Opera Houses, while laudable initiatives in support of the Arts, have tended to promote and subsidise the preferred social activities of the privileged élite. The lottery therefore redistributes income in a regrettable direction – the fond dreams of the poor are funding the leisure pursuits of the rich.

9. The lottery pressurises the vulnerable

There is no escaping the allure of the lottery. Not only is it advertised in the commercial media, but the lottery is the only business allowed to be promoted regularly on the BBC, since the weekly lottery show is nothing other than a prolonged, glitzy ad, complete with 'product endorsements' from each week's star guests. The smiling faces of the big winners are seen in the newspapers and on TV, and they become a further incitement to buy more tickets.

When betting shops were licensed in the sixties, careful restrictions were set in place to prevent excessive gambling, so that even now it is impossible to see in through the windows, and children are kept out. Lottery tickets, however, can be bought at almost every newsagent and supermarket. The instant scratch cards are always available and the unrestricted size of the rollover prizes provokes a Saturday afternoon fever as long queues of gamblers wait to spend more money than they can afford. The cycle is self-fuelling: the more they spend, the larger the prize and so the greater the temptation to spend too much again the next week.

Post-lottery syndrome is how some doctors now describe Saturday nights after the lottery results have been announced. Some who have failed yet again to choose the winning numbers are plunged into gloom and console themselves by drinking too heavily. The constant glare of lottery publicity has also brought immense pressure to bear upon those who are susceptible to compulsive gambling. In one recent case, a woman who had run a sub post office and village shop for twenty-three years was prosecuted for stealing scratch cards between May 1995 and February 1996. In a moment of weakness she had removed the foil from a scratch card without paying for it. Before she knew it she was hooked, eventually stealing cards worth more than £4,600. To make matters worse, she began fiddling payments to pensioners to try to make up the shortfall. She had never before been in trouble with the law, but lottery fever has brought her disgrace. Tibor Barsony, Executive Director of the Canadian Foundation on Compulsive Gambling, has been bluntly critical of state-sponsored lotteries: 'Governments should go to Gamblers Anonymous. They have become addicted to gambling' (quoted in *Newsweek*, 9 September 1996).

It is regrettable but realistic to conclude that the lottery is here to stay. No government would dream of closing down an activity that is so widely popular and that generates income for the state without being seen as a means of taxation. While the tenth commandment expressly excludes committed Christians from buying lottery tickets and from indulging in any other forms of consumerist excess, we still need to consider appropriate regulations for this immensely popular form of legalised gambling. We conclude that the lottery needs to be regulated more strictly, so that what many describe as their 'harmless flutter' does not continue to provoke a climate of excessive consumerism and national greed.

The following modest proposals would certainly improve the management of a state-sponsored lottery: increase the percentage given to charities to 25%; reverse the decision allowing Camelot to introduce a second weekly draw mid-week; remove the right of Camelot to retain the interest on unclaimed prizes, redirecting this income to charities; in order to restrain excessive lottery fever and to protect the winners themselves, set a ceiling of £1 million as the maximum prize level; close down the instant scratch cards; ensure that the advertising does not give a misleading impression of the chances of a big win; introduce a maximum ticket entitlement per person in any one purchase, thus restricting the amount anyone can conveniently spend on the lottery; since children are not entitled to buy lottery tickets, restrict TV advertising of the lottery until after the 9pm threshold; introduce punitive fines and automatically remove the lottery franchise after one offence from any retailer who illegally sells tickets to children under sixteen.

The cost of coveting

Coveting needs a health warning: obsessive materialism can seriously damage your humanity and health. Life is profoundly diminished when we begin to believe that something only really matters if we can put a price tag upon it. A Texas multi-millionaire unwittingly revealed the extent to which covetousness had withered his life and values when he declared, 'If it don't make money, it ain't pretty.' What price beauty or love, tenderness or compassion? Michael Douglas was given the definitive line in the movie *Wall Street* that summed up the rampant acquisitiveness of the West at the end of the twentieth century: 'Greed is good.'

There's certainly nothing intrinsically wrong with enjoying the benefits of material prosperity, but whenever we lose our sense of proportion, whether as individuals or as a nation, we begin to lose our higher values and diminish ourselves, becoming absorbed in a narrow and driven consumerism. Coveting is the love of acquisitiveness, and in a world driven by coveting, there can never be lasting satisfaction. Enough, for the covetous, can never be enough. There are two kinds of casualties in this dehumanising excess. There are those who are redundant, unemployed or debt-ridden, and there are also those who exult in a consumerist paradise of extravagant wealth and acquisitions. Consumerism is like salt water – the more you have, the more you want.

Afterword

Jesus and the Commandments

It would take another book to do credit to the richness of Jesus' ethical teaching, but before this book closes we need to turn for a moment to consider Jesus' approach to the Ten Commandments.

Jesus took the commandments further than anyone else. In the Sermon on the Mount he turned a searchlight upon our innermost secrets. He intensified the law against unlawful killing so that it was even made to oppose the hidden hatred or bitterness that would never find expression in actual murderous acts. The law against adultery was extended so that it not only condemned adulterous escapades but also lustful fantasies concealed in the heart. It would be absurd for the laws of a nation to be concerned with our inner condition in such a way, but Jesus' concern was twofold in his proclamation of uncompromising purity of heart. He invited his followers to recognise the perfect correlation between the content of his teaching and the manner of his life. He also invited them to search their hearts and discover their own essential selfishness. No one except Jesus could hope to fulfil his ethical teaching.

In his summary of the law, Jesus endorsed the Old Testament summaries: to love God with all that we are and to love our neighbour as ourselves. He added three new love commands. His followers should love one another as he had loved them, love their enemies, and demonstrate their love for Jesus by keeping his commandments.

Jesus' ethic is not simply a catalogue of excesses to avoid, but an invitation to embark on an alternative lifestyle. The centre of gravity for this new way of living is self-giving love, first to God and then to one another. Jesus was unmistakably full of life and full of purity, and so his own life stands as a persuasive proof that the way of love that he taught and lived opens up new possibilities of 'abundant life' that can never be found through self-indulgence.

The first Christians came to understand that the crucifixion of Jesus was inevitable. His purity of heart exposed the hypocrisy of the religious and political leaders of the day. Their darkness despised his light and so they did all in their power to extinguish him. The historical resurrection of Jesus is the triumph of purity, the definitive victory of the self-giving love of God.

The cross was also seen to be necessary in a second way. Jesus' life and teaching demonstrated our shortcomings and the universal condition of impurity of heart. His death was much more than his rejection by corrupt leaders; it was also an atoning sacrifice, in which he became our substitute, paying the price for our selfish living and providing the opportunity for a fresh start. Jesus Christ is therefore so much more than a good example. To those who put their trust in him and in his death on our behalf, he offers the gifts of forgiveness, a new access to the love of God, and new possibilities of inner renewal through the indwelling presence of the Holy Spirit.

The Ten Commandments provide the necessary framework for a decent and civilised society. If we are to avoid drifting any further towards the death of our civilisation, the Ten Commandments need to be seen once again as a sure foundation for wise living. They provide a coherent framework to keep at bay the destructive forces of selfishness, anarchy and decay.

Jesus complements the wisdom of the commandments by inviting all who choose to follow him to walk his way of love and seek his purity of heart. He is the Lord of love and the Giver of hope. Just as the Ten Commandments provide a secure foundation for society, Jesus provides the possibility of inner transformation. When we give our lives to Christ, we can experience his presence and begin to be inwardly renewed by the self-giving love of God.

Selected Bibliography

The most penetrating and enduring explorations in the English language of the moral implications of the Ten Commandments are found in Shakespeare and Chaucer, and in the great tradition of the English novel, through Fielding, Richardson and Defoe and then into the glories of the nineteenth century, beginning with Jane Austen and then continuing with the Brontë sisters, George Eliot and Charles Dickens. What follows is no more than a selected bibliography, indicating some possible starting points for further study and illumination.

Christian Aid, *Pennies from Seven*, Christian Aid, 1995.

C. Achebe, *Things Fall Apart*, Heinemann, 1958.

P. Adams, *Odious Debt*, Earthscan, 1991.

M. Amis, *London Fields*, Jonathan Cape, 1989.

J. Anderson, *Issues of Life and Death*, Hodder, 1976.

D. Atkinson and D. Field (eds), *New Dictionary of Christian Ethics and Pastoral Theology*, IVP, 1994.

D. Atkinson, *Peace in Our Time?*, IVP, 1985.

—— *Pastoral Ethics*, Lion, 1994.

S. Beckett, *Waiting for Godot*, Faber, 1956.

—— *Endgame*, Faber, 1958.

—— *Happy Days*, Faber, 1963.

—— *Collected Shorter Plays*, Faber, 1984.

C. Berry, *The Rites of Life: Christians and Bio-Medical Decision Making*, Hodder, 1987.

B. Bryson, *Notes from a Small Island*, Doubleday, 1995.

N. de S. Cameron and P. Sims, *Abortion: The Crisis in Morals and Medicine*, IVP, 1986.

M. Cassidy, *The Politics of Love*, Hodder, 1991.

—— *A Witness for Ever*, Hodder, 1995.

F. Catherwood, *The Christian in Industrial Society*, IVP, 1980.

J. Chang, *Wild Swans*, Collins, 1991.

J. Childress and J. Macquarrie (eds), *A New Dictionary of Christian Ethics*, SCM, 1986.

Church of England Board for Social Responsibility, *The Church and the Bomb*, Hodder, 1982.

K. Clark, *Civilisation*, BBC, 1969.

R. Clark, *Freud*, Granada, 1982.

J. Conrad, *Heart of Darkness*, Dent, 1902.

D. Cook, *The Moral Maze*, SPCK, 1983.

—— *Dilemmas of Life*, IVP, 1990.

—— *Living in the Kingdom: The Ethics of Jesus*, Hodder, 1992.

C. Darwin, *The Origin of Species*, Mentor, 1958.

F. Dostoyevsky, *Crime and Punishment*, Penguin, 1991.

U. Eco, *The Name of the Rose*, Secker & Warburg, 1983.

T.S. Eliot, *Collected Poems 1909–62*, Faber, 1974.

J. Ellul, *The Political Illusion*, Vintage Books, 1972.

F.S. Fitzgerald, *The Great Gatsby*, Everyman, 1991.

J. Fletcher, *Situation Ethics*, SCM, 1966.

G. Flaubert, *Madame Bovary*, Penguin, 1950.

N. Geisler, *Christian Ethics: Options and Issues*, IVP, 1990.

E. Gibbon, *The Decline and Fall of the Roman Empire* (first published 1776–88), Everyman, 1993.

J. Gladwin (ed.), *Dropping the Bomb*, Hodder, 1985.

A. Glyn-Jones, *Holding up a Mirror – how civilizations decline*, Century, 1996.

W. Golding, *Lord of the Flies*, Faber, 1954.

—— *The Spire*, Faber, 1964.

—— *Rites of Passage*, Faber, 1980.

E. Gosse, *Father and Son*, Heinemann, 1907.

R. Graves, *Goodbye to All That*, Penguin, 1960.

G. Greene, *Brighton Rock*, Heinemann, 1938.

M. Green, *Thank God It's Monday*, SU, 1994.

T. Hardy, *Tess of the d'Urbervilles*, MacMillan, 1912.

—— *Jude the Obscure*, MacMillan, 1912.

N. Hawthorne, *The Scarlet Letter*, Everyman, 1906.

J. Heller, *Catch 22*, Cape, 1962.

J. Hersey, *Hiroshima*, Penguin, 1946.

R. Higgins, *The Seventh Enemy*, Hodder, 1978.

A. Holmes, *Ethics: Approaching Moral Decisions*, IVP, 1984.

A. Huxley, *Brave New World*, Chatto & Windus, 1932.

K. Innes, *Caring for the Earth*, Grove, 1991.

H. James, *What Maisie Knew*, Scribner, 1897.

—— *The Portrait of a Lady*, Penguin, 1963.

S. Jenkins, *Newspapers – The Power and the Money*, Faber, 1979.

D. Jones, *In Parenthesis*, Faber, 1937.

D. G. Jones, *Brave New People: Ethical Issues at the Commencement of Life*, IVP, 1984.

—— *Manufacturing Humans: The Challenge of the New Reproductive Technologies*, IVP, 1987.

F. Kafka, *The Castle*, Secker & Warburg, 1930.

—— *The Trial*, Gollancz, 1935.

—— *Stories 1904–24*, MacDonald, 1981.

C. Kerr, *The Way of Peace: Peace amidst the conflict in Northern Ireland*, Hodder, 1990.

M. Kidton and R. Segal (eds), *The New State of the World Atlas*, Simon & Schuster, 1991.

M. L. King, *Strength to Love*, Hodder, 1964.

A. Koestler, *Darkness at Noon*, Penguin, 1947.

D. Kraybill, *The Upside Down Kingdom*, Herald, 1978.

A. Kreider, *Towards Holiness*, Marshalls, 1986.

M. Kundera, *The Unbearable Lightness of Being*, Faber, 1984.

M. Langford, *The Good and the True: An Introduction to Christian Ethics*, SCM, 1985.

P. Larkin, *Collected Poems*, Faber, 1988.

J. Lasserre, *War and the Gospel*, James Clarke, 1962.

D.H. Lawrence, *Women in Love*, Secker, 1921.

—— *Sons and Lovers*, Cambridge, 1992 (original text).

F. Leboyer, *La Sacre de la Naissance*, Phebus, 1982.

S. Lees (ed.), *The Role of Women*, IVP, 1984.

P. Levi, *If This Is a Man*, Orion, 1960.

——— *The Periodic Table*, Michael Joseph, 1985.

D. Lodge, *Changing Places*, Secker & Warburg, 1975.

——— *Nice Work*, Secker & Warburg, 1988.

A. Lurie, *The War Between the Tates*, Heinemann, 1974.

D. McLellan, *Karl Marx*, Granada, 1976.

D. Mills-Powell (ed.), *Decide for Peace*, Marshalls, 1986.

M. Moynagh, *Making Unemployment Work*, Lion, 1985.

L. Newbigin, *The Gospel in a Pluralist Society*, SPCK, 1989.

F. Nietzsche, *A Nietzsche Reader*, Penguin, 1977.

L. Nilsson, *A Child Is Born*, Dell, 1977.

J. Oberski, *A Childhood*, Hodder, 1983.

O. O'Donovan, *The Christian and the Unborn Child*, Grove, 1975.

G. Orwell, *Animal Farm*, Secker & Warburg, 1945.

——— *Nineteen Eighty-Four*, Secker & Warburg, 1949.

L. Osborn, *Guardians of Creation*, IVP, 1993.

W. Owen, *The Poems*, Penguin, 1985.

V. Packard, *The Hidden Persuaders*, Penguin, 1981.

B. Pasternak, *Doctor Zhivago*, Collins, 1958.

A. Pettifor, *Debt, the Most Potent Form of Slavery*, Christian Aid, 1995.

C. Ponting, *The Right to Know*, Sphere, 1985.

H. Rookmaaker, *Modern Art and the Death of a Culture*, IVP, 1970.

J. Sachs, *Understanding Shock Therapy*, Social Market Foundation, 1994.

A. Sampson, *The Arms Bazaar*, Hodder, 1977.

——— *The Money Lenders*, Hodder, 1981.

——— *The Changing Anatomy of Britain*, Hodder, 1982.

——— *The Essential Anatomy of Britain*, Hodder, 1992.

——— ed. *North and South*, The Brandt Report, Pan, 1980.

J.P. Sartre, *Nausea*, Penguin, 1967.

——— *Words*, Faber, 1983.

S. Sassoon, *The War Poems*, Faber, 1983.

F. Schaeffer, *The God Who Is There*, Hodder, 1968.

——— *How Should We Then Live?*, Revell, 1976.

M. Schluter and D. Lee, *The R Factor*, Hodder, 1993.

E. Schumacher, *Small Is Beautiful*, Blond & Briggs, 1973.

D. Sheppard, *Bias to the Poor*, Hodder, 1983.

R. Sider, *Christ and Violence*, Herald, 1979.

R. Sider and R. Taylor, *Nuclear Holocaust and Christian Hope*, Hodder, 1983.

R. Sider and O. O'Donovan, *Peace and War: A Debate about Pacifism*, Grove, 1985.

R. Sider (ed.), *Living More Simply*, Hodder, 1980.

R. Sider, *Rich Christians in an Age of Hunger*, Hodder, 1990.

T. Sine, *The Mustard Seed Conspiracy*, Word, 1981.

—— *Wild Hope*, Marshalls, 1992.

J. Sire, *The Universe Next Door*, IVP, 1976.

L. Smedes, *Mere Morality*, Lion, 1983.

A. Solzhenitzyn, *One Day in the Life of Ivan Denizovitch*, Gollancz, 1963.

—— *One Word of Truth*, Bodley Head, 1972.

A. Storkey, *The Meanings of Love*, IVP, 1994.

E. Storkey, *What's Right with Feminism?*, SPCK, 1985.

J. Stott, *Issues Facing Christians Today*, Marshalls, 1990.

Suetonius, *The Twelve Caesars*, Penguin, 1957.

P. Theroux, *The Kingdom by the Sea*, Hamish Hamilton, 1983.

E. Thompson and D. Smith (eds), *Protest and Survive*, Penguin, 1980.

L. Tolstoy, *Anna Karenina*, Everyman, 1992.

—— *War and Peace*, Everyman, 1992.

J. Updike, *Marry Me*, Penguin, 1977.

—— *Hugging the Shore*, Penguin, 1985.

P. Vardy, *Business Morality*, Marshalls, 1989.

K. Vonnegut, *Slaughterhouse 5*, Triad/Panther, 1979.

T. Walter, *Hope on the Dole*, SPCK, 1985.

J. Wallis, *Agenda for Biblical People*, Harper & Row, 1976.

—— *The Call to Conversion*, Lion, 1981.

D. Wells, *God in the Wasteland*, IVP, 1994.

J. White, *Money Isn't God*, IVP, 1993.

C. Wright, *Living as the People of God*, IVP, 1983.

W.B. Yeats, *Collected Poems*, MacMillan, 1982.

J. Yoder, *The Politics of Jesus*, Eerdmans, 1972.

—— *The Original Revolution*, Herald, 1977.

J. Yoder (ed., with Hutterite Brethren), *God's Revolution: the witness of Ebehard Arnold*, Paulist Press, 1984.

Y. Zamyatin, *We*, Jonathan Cape, 1970.

E. Zola, *Therese Raquin*, Penguin, 1962.

—— *La Bete Humaine*, Penguin, 1977.

—— *Germinal*, Everyman, 1991.